A motivating and inspiring set of believable and practical strateg[...] into entertaining and powerful stories. *Tape Breakers* opens your eyes to how important you are to the people in your life and how you can escalate your impact and influence.
—Bruce A. Tollner, co-founder, Rep 1 Sports and co-author of *Sidelined: Overcoming Odds through Unity, Passion, and Perseverance* with Chuck Pagano and Tony Dungy.

Jim is inspiring and motivating. *Tape Breakers* is a must read for anyone who wants to succeed.
—Teemu Selanne, Stanley Cup Champion, 10-time NHL All-Star, six-time Olympian, four-time Olympic medalist.

At the end of the race how will you measure your time? Have you ever thought about what race you're in? Jim Akers has signed up to be your coach. All you have to do is pick up, *Tape Breakers*, and you'll hear the starters pistol on the first page.
—W Mitchell, Speakers Hall of Fame, Author of, *It's Not What Happens To You, It's What You Do About It.*

On *American Ninja Warrior*, everyone wants to reach the top of the mountain. But just like in life, how they handle the obstacles and adversity along the way defines their race. *Tape Breakers* will help you live out the most important roles in your life with courage, conviction, and commitment. Jim lays out a wonderful blueprint for climbing the mountains in your life and finishing strong.
—Akbar Gbaja-Biamila, American Ninja Warrior co-host, NFL Network analyst, and former NFL player.

Akers uses the running metaphor like a great coach, encouraging us to use our time, talents and resources more effectively. Take his *Tape Breakers* strategies to heart to produce more joy, happiness and success in your life.
—Don Kardong, 1976 U. S. Olympian, winner of Honolulu Marathon, member Inland Empire Sports Hall of Fame, and Founder Lilac Bloomsday Run.

I have known Jim for a decade and have experienced the impact of his leadership in business, with his family and in his community. In Tape Breakers, Jim lays out

the path to lasting success. Anyone who has been fortunate enough to spend time with Jim has learned from him and his example of servant leadership. You will live a life with more impact after reading Tape Breakers and following his advice!
—Tom Koos, CEO, Weber-Stephens Products

Clear, practical, and powerful—Jim goes beyond motivation. *Tape Breakers* will help anyone raise their game and positively expand their influence.
—Robb Nen, World Series Champion, three-time National League All-Star

Give your dreams a boost and increase your ability to follow through and meet more of your goals with Jim's book *Tape Breakers*. It's a great source of encouragement and practical strategies sure to help everyone.
—Tom Sneva, 1983 Indianapolis 500 winner and three-time runner-up, two-time USAC National Champion, member Motorsports Hall of Fame.

Jim is one who has been there and done the right things. In *Tape Breakers* he shares the elements of successful living and achieving. And he attributes his learnings and lessons from some of the greats in his life. Outstanding work, demonstrating what he preaches and, more importantly, practices. Great stuff!
—Charles A. 'Chuck' Coonradt, founder of The Game of Work, speaker, and author of *The Game of Work*, *Managing the Obvious* and *The Four Laws of Debt Free Prosperity*

For anyone who really wants to live life the way the Lord created us to live—one filled with "Purpose" and "Impact"—*Tape Breakers* shows you how. Jim has provided an awesome framework to help guide and motivate you towards what matters most in life – People!
—Scott Westering, Head Football Coach, Pacific Lutheran University, member PLU Hall of Fame, All-American on 1980 NAIA national title team

*Tape Breakers* is motivating, inspiring, and powerful. Jim converted years of incredible experience into a toolbox of resources sure to raise your performance and help you make a lasting difference in the lives of the people you care about most.
—George Raveling, Nike's Director of International Basketball, member College Basketball, & Naismith Memorial Basketball Hall of Fame

# Tape
# Breakers

Don,

Look forward to
running great races
with you.

Jami Atkers

ROMANS 8:28

# Tape Breakers

**MAXIMIZE YOUR IMPACT WITH PEOPLE YOU LOVE, TEAMS YOU LEAD, AND CAUSES THAT STIR YOUR HEART**

Jim Akers

ISBN: 1943526133
ISBN 13: 9781943526130
Library of Congress Control Number: 2015918640
Author Academy Elite, Powell, OH

The Internet addresses in this book are accurate at the time of publication. They are provided as a resource. Jim Akers or the publisher do not endorse them or vouch for their content or permanence.

# Contents

# Foreward

Impact is an interesting phenomenon.

In some ways we all impact each other. But the more important question is what type of impact are we creating? And is that impact big or small—positive or negative?

Throughout his career as a successful businessman, Jim Akers created impact upon the people he loved, the teams he led, and the causes that stirred his heart. Yet in recent years Jim wanted to take impact to a whole new level. And so he centered his life on this quest—discovering how to increase positive impact upon others.

As a result, Jim Akers started *Impactful Notes* to encourage success "one note at a time." He accomplished this goal by delivering inspirational, encouraging, motivational and principle-based notes to help people unlock their potential and achieve their dreams.

The "inspiration" behind *Impactful Notes* grew out of a personal quest to stay connected with his teenaged boys when they were about to start high school. Knowing that high school offered greater independence and they would face new and challenging academic, social and athletic situations, he began writing and texting notes of inspiration, encouragement, motivation and wisdom every morning.

The notes hit the mark with his sons, so the boys shared the messages with their friends, who shared them with their friends. Jim started texting the notes to colleagues, friends and other family members. The impact and success of the daily notes continued to grow. Thus, *Impactful Notes* was born. Before he knew it, Jim was sending notes to hundreds of people. And now, many years later *Impactful Notes* continues its mission to encourage and inspire peak performance.

Jim distilled decades of personal and professional lessons into this resource *Tape Breakers*. It's a proven plan that increase your impact because it shows you how to:

- Identify and focus on achieving success that can't be lost or taken away.
- Avoid the trap that will rob you of vital time, energy and resources.
- Increase your impact on and influence with the most important people in your life.
- Surround yourself with the people and resources that high achievers use to stay focused on running the races that give you the greatest opportunity for impact and influence.
- Employ effective tools and ways of thinking to get back on track when you are feeling empty, frustrated and disillusioned.

Blending a mix of stories, research and personal experience, Jim shares a race plan that will guide you to finish strong—to positively impact people you love, teams you lead and causes that stir your heart.

Isn't it time you ran the race of your choosing—one that changes lives, inspires hearts and unlocks exciting new possibilities?

Kary Oberbrunner
CEO of Redeem the Day and Igniting Souls
Co-creator of Author Academy Elite
Author of *Day Job to Dream Job, The Deeper Path, and Your Secret Name*

# PART 1

## On Your Mark!

### "Identifying the Race"

> *"There are few things more powerful than a life lived with passionate clarity."*
> —Irwin McManus

> *"The goal is not just long life, or even a prosperous one; it's to make a meaningful life out of an ordinary one."*
> —Peter Drucker

# CHAPTER 1

# Life is all About Impact: "An Unlikely Source of Clarity"

*"It is no use walking anywhere to preach unless our walking is*
*our preaching."*
—ST. FRANCIS OF ASSISI

*"A life is not important except in the impact it has on other*
*lives."*
—JACKIE ROBINSON

I expected it. And because I knew it was coming, I had plenty of time to think about it. Still, I didn't know how I'd respond. No one ever does.

When I awoke, it was just another workday. No thought required, I functioned predominantly on autopilot. The habit of routine guided my every move. I turned to the mirror to confirm everything was in place. The last task in my mindless ritual required me to clip my phone to my belt. But before I could, the phone rang. I pulled it out to see who was calling—it was my mom.

I froze for a moment, but it continued to ring. "Do I want to answer this?" I thought. "Or should I just let it go to voicemail?"

I knew what I had to do. I took a deep breath and pushed the button to take the call. I think I mustered up a weak, "Good morning, Mom." There were a couple seconds of silence that felt like minutes as I could hear her collecting herself. "Jim," and she started to cry, "Your dad passed away this morning."

I don't remember anything else she said. She may have still been talking when I said, "I love you, Mom. I will call you later today," and hung up. I stood in the closet motionless. My normal thoughtless routine had been interrupted and now I wasn't sure what I was supposed to do next.

My head was spinning. You know that feeling when you're not sure of what to do next. It was like I had just been blindsided by a massive body blow. I quickly came to realize that even when you expect bad news you don't feel its magnitude until it actually happens. I felt lightheaded and lowered myself to my knees. "Now what?" I thought. Shaken and unsure, my mind began flashing to thoughts of seeing my dad for the last time.

It had just been a couple short weeks since I walked into the intensive care unit (ICU) at Sacred Heart Medical Center in Spokane, Washington. There was a silent urgency you could feel. Peering in the rooms and seeing an abundance of tubes and monitors was not comforting. Dad's health had taken a turn for the worse, and he was entering his third week in the ICU. My brother and sister warned me, but it was unsettling to actually realize Dad was unable to speak or communicate. A rush of emotion rose up in me when the medical staff said they didn't think he was aware of what was going on around him.

## Saying goodbye

In the evening Mom and I ate dinner in the hospital cafeteria. Telling stories about Dad, their life together and our family helped revitalize her spirits—great memories can do that. After dinner she headed home for much-needed rest, and I returned to Dad's room to wrestle with the perplexing reality of his condition. I slept lightly in the chair next to his bedside for five nights. We never left him alone. He would've told us to go home, but I would've gladly ignored his directions.

Every night, he became unsettled—calling out names and reliving events from his past. Our presence in the room seemed to soothe and comfort him like a warm blanket. I was never sure he knew it was me who was there, but it really didn't matter. When I held his hand and looked in his eyes, I felt he knew it was me.

My emotions were tattered and bruised after five days. You know the feeling when you're clinging tightly to something you can't keep. It was on Mom's mind when we sat down for dinner that last night. She wasn't going to come out and say it. Goodness, she didn't even want to think it. But as we talked she told stories about Dad and me. She wanted to make sure I understood that this night may be the last time I would see my dad.

I kissed my mom, hugged her tightly, and sent her home. As I walked back to the ICU, the weight of my dad's race coming to an end was emotionally overwhelming. You don't easily see the depth, complexity and importance of how you run your race until you think deeply about someone you love approaching the finish line. You begin to gain some missing clarity. A seemingly unlikely source of clarity.

As I sat down in the chair, I was numb to the physical fatigue that gripped me. Dad was particularly restless that night. I remember rubbing his back, holding his hand and being keenly aware of nearly every minute that ticked off the clock.

When 4 am arrived, I prepared to leave for the airport by getting dressed, brushing my teeth and packing my bags. No shower—a little deodorant would have to do. I was struggling to pull myself away from his bedside when I reached out one last time to hold his hand. I looked at his frail body in disbelief that this was the man I called Dad. I wrapped my hands around his hand and squeezed softly. I reached up and stroked the hair on his head, and his eyes opened slowly. I squeezed his hand again and he smiled. A magnificent smile that brought me to tears!

I think he knew. I don't know how. I don't know why, but he knew. As I held his hand and enjoyed his smile, he weakly squeezed my hand. He was lovingly saying goodbye. I leaned over and kissed him on the forehead and said, "I love you, Dad!" He closed his eyes and I quickly gathered my things. I headed to the car without slowing down as I walked past the nurses' station. I didn't want anything to disturb this final memory.

## Weaving the race together

From the moment I walked out of the hospital every time my phone rang I cautiously peeked to identify the caller. My faith in the possibility of a miracle kept me from thinking about my dad crossing the finish line for the final time, but I had only been back home for a few days when Mom's call came. Now I was on the floor in my closet, fighting back tears and wishing this was just a bad dream.

By worldly standards, he was an ordinary man. But the stories of this seemingly ordinary life, woven together, showed me that the marathon we call life is truly a collection of many races. I didn't know much about my dad's story growing up. I largely drew from what I observed and then filled in many of the missing pieces as I prepared to speak at his funeral. Races of opportunity and challenge, victory and defeat, love and heartbreak, and infinite possibilities to positively impact the people he loved, the teams he led and the causes that stirred his heart.

> "God must love ordinary men, because he created so many of them."
> —Abraham Lincoln

Dad was a man of very few words. He exemplified the old adage that success is "walking the talk" with a twist. He didn't talk; instead he just walked. He walked and lived with unbridled commitment and conviction. Abraham Lincoln said, "God must love ordinary men, because he created so many of them." It shouldn't amaze you that ordinary becomes extraordinary if you will just keep walking.

Much of my dad's life didn't make sense or feel pleasant. In fact, in many ways it was tragic and included many challenging and difficult races. He grew up the youngest of five children, in abject poverty, in the Appalachian mountains of West Virginia. When he was five, his 13-year-old sister Mary was killed in a car accident. The following year his brother Robert died of rheumatic heart failure. The heartbreak of these losses led his mother to suffer a nervous breakdown and crushed his father's spirit. Although a promising athlete, he struggled as a student—barely making his way to graduation. College was not an option for my dad.

Like many young men in West Virginia, he went to work in the coalmines. After only a few days, his older brother Albert, out of concern for my dad's health and safety, didn't let him return to the mines. Abe, always looking to do what was best for his little brother, helped him enlist in the Air Force.

Shortly after starting his military career, Dad's first wife tragically died just months after giving birth to their first child, my half-sister Debbie. He left his infant daughter with his family while he continued his military service requirements, eventually reuniting with Debbie after marrying my mom. He served two tours of overseas combat duty and returned to West Virginia only once to see his ailing mother who did not remember him.

Chip Ingram, the best-selling author of *Good to Great in God's Eyes*, sums up the race of life well. He says, "God's ultimate purposes for our lives are often achieved by circumstances that seem to make no 'apparent' sense to us."[1] You don't always know the good your races are intended to produce until you run them with conviction.

On the day of my dad's funeral, I thought about the races he ran. How did he even get started? Why didn't he quit? Where did he gain the strength to persevere and accelerate? I had never stepped back to think about the view from the final finish line. When you stand on the finish line and look backwards, you begin to realize your desire for a great legacy runs deep—you want to be remembered for running an impactful race. You want your race to matter.

## The race comes into view

The first thing I remember about my dad's funeral was the burial. After the Words of Institution, a short distance from the site, a single trumpeter played "Taps" and a 21-gun salute rang out. As the casket was lowered into the grave, the six-member military honor guard carefully removed the American flag from the casket. The honor guard snapped the flag and began to fold it with 12 precise folds that commanded the full attention of everyone present.

They made the last meticulous fold, leaving the stars pointing upward—a reminder of our nation's motto, "In God We Trust." Then the head of the honor guard pulled the flag close to his chest as the remainder of the honor guard raised their arms in salute. I stood behind my mom as he approached and kneeled down in front of her. He extended the flag to my mom, and said, "On behalf of the President of the United States, the United States Air Force, and a grateful nation, please accept this flag as a symbol of appreciation for Master Sergeant James Akers' honorable and faithful service. God bless you and this family, and God Bless the United States of America."

The second thing I remember about Dad's funeral was looking out from the pulpit in the church and seeing it overflowing with people. How is it that this seemingly private and ordinary man could have such a positive impact on so many people? How is it that he could finish this marathon of life so well? There were so many events along the way that should have kept him from starting new races, let alone finding the courage and stamina to finish what he had already started. How do you take a seemingly ordinary life and deliver extraordinary impact?

He finished a 22-year career as a noncommissioned officer in the Air Force, started a new career, loved and cherished my mom for over 45 years of marriage, figured out how to get three kids through college without ever taking a loan, and always had something in his pocket when someone asked for help. Digging through the few pictures and keepsakes he had stashed away I saw medals of commendation, articles of tribute and appreciation and cards of thanks from people who I know were complete strangers.

How could I have missed what was right in front of my eyes all these years? I had been reading, studying and writing about success for years and never made this critical connection to our races. I read the biographies of Abraham Lincoln, Harry Truman, Thomas Edison, C. S. Lewis, Arnold Palmer, Andrew Carnegie, Margaret Thatcher, Walt Disney, Bill Gates, Thomas Jefferson, Andy Grove, Walter Cronkite, Billy Graham, Ronald Reagan, Ben Hogan, Albert Einstein and dozens more and not once thought about them alongside Dad's story. Not until now had I thought about them alongside your story.

## It's all about impact

I shouldn't have been surprised. Once again it was not what Dad said but ultimately what I observed. Great and lasting impact is not reserved for those who are placed on a grand and opulent stage. Impact does not wait for the size of your audience to grow. Impact does not require you to look for a better venue to run. Impact results from intentionally directing the stewardship of your time, talent and resources towards touching and changing lives. Impact is about becoming the hero of your race.

I have wondered what would've happened if Dad hadn't run his race. What if he didn't accept his role of hero in his own race? The view from the finish line changes everything. It begs you to think forward. What will be lost if you don't run the courageous race? Who will be left behind? Who will miss your intended contribution if *you* don't run for impact?

Life is a marathon, and the story you write will ultimately reflect how you run the many seemingly small races in your life. Positive life-changing impact is the result of running the difficult races regardless of the challenges and obstacles. Impact is pouring all of yourself into breaking the tape—finishing strong.

Elie Wiesel, in his best-selling book *Souls on Fire*, captures the view of the finish line well when he writes, "When we die and go to Heaven and we meet our Maker, we are not going to be asked why did you not become a messiah, why did you not discover a cure for such and such. The only thing you are going to be asked at that precious moment is, 'Why did you not become you?'"

The race of life is all about impact. Picking, running and breaking the tape in races that positively change lives. You have been created to fulfill a great purpose. No one has your unique place in history to positively impact the people you love, the teams you lead and the causes that stir your heart. No one! Becoming you is born, nurtured and completed in the pursuit of pouring your heart and soul into creating positive impact every day in the lives of people who need your love and care.

> "God has given us two incredible things; absolutely awesome ability and freedom of choice. The tragedy is that, for the most part, many of us have refused them both."
> —Frank Donnelly

Everyone writes a story with their race. Run a race that weaves together a story bold enough and big enough to change lives, inspire hearts and unlock possibilities.

Today is a great day to find the starting line and embrace being the hero of your race—On your mark!

# CHAPTER 2

# It's a Trap: "Looking for the Starting Line in all the Wrong Places"

*"Perseverance is not a long race: It is many short races one after another."*
—W*ALTER* E*LLIOT*

*"Men lust, but they know not what for. They fight and compete, but they forget the prize; they spread seed, but spurn the seasons of growth; they chase power and glory, but miss the meaning of life."*
—G*EORGE* G*ILDER*

"On your mark, get set, go!" Familiar words to anyone who has run a race. "On your mark" is the call alerting racers to step up to the starting line. But what if you line up for the wrong race? What if you heard the call "On your mark," and even though it didn't look like the right race, you ran anyway?

Driving to what she thought was the starting line for a prestigious invitational road race, a world-class runner got lost. But after stopping to ask for help, she was directed to a location she thought fit the description of the starting line.

Anxious she would miss the call to the starting line, she was relieved to see runners still gathering in the parking lot when she finally arrived. She quickly laced up her shoes and headed to the registration table. The race official greeted her with exuberant excitement when she gave them her name. They had not expected a world-class runner to participate. She was surprised they did not have a record of her entry, but they quickly prepared her a racing bib, pinned it to her singlet and directed her to the starting line.

In spite of the rush and confusion, she ran a comfortable race and won easily. Maybe it was the early jolt of adrenaline that propelled her to the finish line four minutes ahead of the entire field. But after the race, when she was expecting an envelope with prize money, to go along with the first place medal hanging around her neck, she realized she had stepped up to the wrong starting line.[1] There were two road races in the area that morning. She ran in the wrong race.

## Where Are You Going?

You don't intentionally step up to the wrong starting line. But life is a complex marathon made up of a collection of races that can find you looking for the starting line in all the wrong places. In Lewis Carroll's wonderful fairy tale, *Alice in Wonderland*, Alice gets lost, comes upon the Cheshire Cat, and asks, "Would you tell me, please, which way I ought to go from here?" "That depends a good deal on where you want to get to," said the Cat. "I don't much care where," said Alice. "Then it doesn't matter which way you go," said the Cat. "So long as I get somewhere," Alice added as an explanation. "Oh, you're sure to do that," said the Cat, "if you only walk long enough."[2]

Where do you want to get to? You may not always know where you want to get to, but I know you want to run a successful race. No one intentionally chooses failure. But what if you run the wrong race? What if your race for success is really a trap—welcoming you to the starting line and then sucking all of the meaningful impact out of your race. You can see the Cheshire Cat grinning and saying, "Oh, you're sure to do that if you are lured into the trap."

The goal of a winning race is to use your unique gifts and talents to positively impact the people you love, the teams you lead, and the causes that stir in your heart. Winning the race begins with stepping up to a starting line filled with the potential for positive impact when you hear the call, "On your mark."

# Making the Complex Simple

Charles Schulz used his comic strip, *Peanuts*, to make seemingly complex life issues and circumstances easy to understand. The *Peanuts* characters would reguarly appear at Lucy's "5 cent" psychiatry stand, looking for counsel and advice. Leaning on the counter with his chin in his hand was where Charlie Brown sought answers to life's biggest questions.

One day Charlie Brown dropped a nickel in Lucy's jar. "Okay, Charlie Brown," Lucy shrugged, "what seems to be the problem?" Charlie Brown begins to tell Lucy how he doesn't understand success. Charlie laments that he just doesn't know which race to choose. As he continues to describe his dilemma, Lucy smugly interrupts him and says, "Charlie Brown, imagine a cruise ship. Some people take their deck chairs and set them up in front of the ship so they can see where they are going. And some people set their deck chairs up in the back of the boat so they can see where they have been. Charlie Brown, where would you set your deck chair up?" Charlie Brown thinks for a moment, scratches his head, looks up at Lucy and says, "Lucy, I can't even get my deck chair open."

Lucy was challenging Charlie Brown to pick a starting line—to define success. Regardless of our age, gender, where we start, the races we choose to run or where our races take us, we all want to be successful. But what is success? Typing "success" into a search engine produces over one billion web pages, 102 million videos, 112,000 books and more images than you can even begin to scroll through. Webster defines success as "the accomplishment of an aim or purpose." Lucy defines success as setting your deck chair up with a view.

# Setting Up Your Deck Chair

How do you define success? Everyone eventually wrestles with defining success. One of my most memorable discussions about success was with a group of young men I was coaching. I remember gathering these six young men around my dining room table just prior to their freshman year in high school. It was exciting to get them thinking about their futures.

I got things rolling by telling the story of Charlie Brown and his deck chair. Then I said, "Let's focus on where you are going." I handed them a journal and asked them to open it up. I had personalized each of the journals with their name and made the first entry—"My Dream List," followed with lines numbered up to 100.

The instructions were simple. Write down everything you dream of being, doing and achieving over the course of your life. Let your imagination run wild. Ignore considering if you think something is possible. This exercise has no boundaries, obstacles or restrictions. Just dream big—no limits on time, money or resources. "Don't stop until you reach 100," I said.

After about 10 minutes, they began looking around the table at each other. "How many dreams have you identified?" I asked. Still a long way from 100, I tried to spur their thinking and imagination. I offered a few more thought primers—"Think about people you would like to meet, places you would like to visit, careers you would like to pursue, things you would like to learn, or contributions you would like to make. Do you want to get married and have a family? Where do you want to live? How do you want to live? Who do you want to help? What are you going to do when you are old?" I might have even asked them to think about what kind of gifts they would want to give me. "That should get things moving," I thought.

Now they were writing and sharing their entries. I tried, unconvincingly, to impress upon them that what anyone else had on their list should have no bearing on their dreams. But, after a couple minutes, a lively conversation erupted as they shared dreams they had entered in their journals. In a matter of minutes they were no longer stuck.

They quickly filled their lists up with the names of exotic sports cars, high-profile celebrity careers, spending time with the rich and famous, watches, video gaming rooms, vacation homes, political appointments and world travel to attend premier sporting and cultural events. Dreams turned to fantasy when one of the boys announced his plans to marry a *Sports Illustrated* swimsuit model.

They were on board and headed to the front of the ship. Deck chairs in hand they were setting their sights on the success trap—a future filled with wealth, power and prestige. Not a surprise for a group of young men with little life experience. But a sobering list when you think that most adults, who should have the benefit of perspective, would create a similarly shallow list of dreams.

So I asked, "If you fulfilled your dreams, would you be happy?" Nearly unanimously they agreed that if they had the things on their list they would be happy.

Like so many, they saw a finish line defined by happiness but were looking for the starting line in all the wrong places. Ponder this question—could success...based on the prestige of your career or profession, how much you earn, the size of your house, the toys you own, and how it all compares to your friends and neighbors...generate happiness?

## It's a Trap!

Dr. Peggy Drexler is an assistant professor of psychology at Cornell University. Dr. Drexler, an expert on the motivators and drivers that determine who we are and what we want, says, "Our views of how men and women define success are shaped by social and cultural expectations."[3] Ask for a description of success and regardless of age or gender, "happiness" is the term most commonly used.[4]

> Defining success as happiness based on things that can be lost or taken away is a trap.

Cultural expectations lead you to believe that your success grows in proportion to the level of wealth, power and prestige you accumulate. Make no mistake...the trap of cultural success is very alluring. Defining success as happiness based on things that can be lost or taken away is a trap.

Tony Campolo, professor emeritus of sociology at Eastern University in Pennsylvania, in his book The Success Fantasy, says, "Sociologists teach us that wealth, power, and prestige express a 'strain to consistency.'" This means that when people possess one of these, they tend to have the other two, also. The wealthy tend to have power and prestige. The powerful usually gain prestige and wealth, and the prestigious are likely to be people of wealth and power. People who have only one of these attributes will seldom be content until they have the other two. In our society, the usual path to success is first to acquire wealth and then gradually gain prestige and power."[5]

You can win the lottery, possess great wealth, buy all of the trappings of success, attract a lot of attention, but would you be successful? You can inherit wealth and pursue a life of leisure and self-indulgence, but would you be successful? You can possess immense wealth and be a pop icon without generating any positive impact, but would you be successful?

## Who Wants to Be Uncool?

Cultural success is a powerful force that is nearly impossible to ignore. You are surrounded by the lure of cultural success and the social expectations to pursue it. The flood of advertising, marketing, and promotion scream for you to step to the starting line and chase the happiness mirage.

Take something as simple as smart phones. Today, what is the likelihood you own a mobile phone that is more than four years old? Okay, you can stop laughing. With a steady stream of commercials announcing the arrival of new models and technology, people will stand in line for hours, even days, to own the most socially-desirable new phones. Even late adopters may be one generation behind but likely not two.

So, could you imagine owning a flip phone? You may be reading this and thinking, "What is a flip phone?" According to the ten-year-old daughter of a friend of mine, it is a sign of being uncool and having unsuccessful parents. My friend wanted her daughter to have a phone for emergencies. She had been begging for a phone, but at ten my friend did not want her to have access to an internet-accessible smartphone. However, she could inexpensively set up an old "flip-phone" to handle emergencies. It was logical, practical and economical but not socially acceptable—uncool. And to think some of you can remember when not having a "flip-phone" was uncool.

Her daughter boldly pointed out, "Old technology is not cool. Don't embarrass me like that." Forget practical necessity; it was just not cool enough. We may laugh, but who hasn't had a few uncool hand-me-downs in their life? My first car was definitely not cool. Come to think of it, neither was my second car.

Culture admires and celebrates cool, but cool is a trap. When you approach the starting line and pick the mark for the cultural success lane, you don't think about crossing the finish line of your final race and being asked, "Why did you not become you?" You don't look forward and think about what kind of impact you will generate.

## Where Will the Race Lead?

In the award-winning film "Race to Nowhere: The Dark Side of America's Achievement Culture," film producer Vicki Abeles depicts the damaging effects that the pursuit of cultural success is having on young students. Increasingly, students are striving to get the best grades, produce the best test scores and do lots of extracurricular activities so they can get into the best colleges, garner high-paying jobs and buy all the prizes along the way.

Students are falsely buying into the belief that achieving anything less than an elite level of performance makes them a failure. Think about the damage this view of success engenders. Instead of pursuing their unique potential and developing a process for starting, accelerating and finishing new races, they are being crushed under the weight of culturally-driven expectations. "Through the testimony of educators, parents and education experts, the film reveals an education system in which cheating has become commonplace; students have become disengaged; stress-related illness, depression and burnout are rampant; and young people arrive at college and the workplace unprepared and uninspired."[6]

## Fill-In-The-Blank

You are being coaxed to set your deck chair up on the trap of cultural success. It is powerful, emotionally attractive, and it is flawed. It leads you to believe that success is an event or purchase you set as a goal, frame as a question and fill-in-the-blank. When I share fill-in-the-blank success statements with people, there are always a few people who proudly can fill in some of the blanks. You may be one of them. There are also people who are intently focused on filling-in-the-blank of one particular statement. Others feel remorse, pain and anguish over failing to fill-in-the-blank.

I am sure you can identify with a few of these fill-in-the-blank success statements.

- When I get promoted to _____, I will be successful.
- When I get into (fill in the name of the college), I will be successful.
- When I buy _____, I will be successful.
- When I win _____, I will be successful.
- I will feel successful when _____.

- When I score _____ on the _____ test I will be successful.
- As soon as I save _____, I will be set.
- When I am on the cover of _____, I will be successful.
- I will love myself when _____.
- When I get invited to _____, I will be successful.
- When I accomplish _____, my dad will finally acknowledge me.
- If _____ doesn't come through, my life will be ruined.
- When I get accepted into _____, I will be successful.
- When I marry _____, my life will be complete.
- I will be successful when I finish _____.
- When I stop _____, I will be successful.
- When I move to _____, I will be successful.

Fill-in-the-blank success statements depict the trap of cultural success. The unfortunate reality is, if you are unable to fill in the blank, you've failed. If you fill-in-the-blank with something less than expected, you didn't measure up. And if you successfully fill-in-the-blank, you will reward yourself with a new blank to take its place.

## It's Easy to Fall

The Greek philosopher Plautus said, "No man is wise enough by himself."—a truth revealed when you rely on your own understanding and fail to learn from the experiences of others. Even when you understand the trap, it does not stop you from falling into it. I passionately associated my success with career progression and advancement.

> "No man is wise enough by himself."
> —Plautus

Shortly before my 50th birthday I celebrated my 25th company anniversary. I was enjoying a great career filled with advancement and rewards. I was still working on filling in the blank. "I will be successful when I become a Senior Vice President." I was motivated by being designated as an HP+—a personnel label indicating I still had a chance to fill in the blank.

Our company was going through a variety of changes that included naming one of my old bosses as president. I had known Tom for years, and he had always been a wonderful career advocate. Tom made a variety of organizational changes. He expanded my role to include scope and geography that had previously carried the title of Senior Vice President. But someone else was named to the Senior Vice President role I coveted.

Walking to our car, after returning from a trip, Tom asked me, "How does it feel to get the job you stated was your career goal?" At that moment all I could think about was the title I didn't get. Tom was right—the scope and responsibility of my new job did reflect my goal, but I wasn't a Senior Vice President.

I am not sure how far we walked before Tom broke the silence by reminding me of a conversation we had about my previously-stated career goal. I struggled to see the correlation because the title was not the same, the compensation was not the same, and the career progression was not the same. But the job responsibilities were what I set my sights on when I set my deck chair up.

Ever gotten what you thought you wanted only to discover you weren't clear enough? All of a sudden I realized my deck chair was perched on the trap. I was pursuing fill-in-the-blank success based on titles, promotions and prestige. At first I didn't want to believe it. But then a visit from one of our human resource leaders removed any doubt. He told me that because of my stated desire to remain in Southern California, for family reasons, my HP+ designation was being removed.

It is so easy to fall into the trap of cultural success. Who doesn't want to be seen as successful? I certainly wanted people to see me as a success. The day I was removed from this exclusive career advancement list my fill-in-the-blank answer was replaced with questions. Why had I worked so hard? Did I run the wrong race? What finish line am I running towards?

The seemingly logical, maybe insidious, progression of fill-in-the-blank statements draws you right into the cultural success trap. The grave danger is falsely believing your race is over when you can no longer fill in the blank. I can assure you the race is not over, but it brings you to a critical question. Are you going to be drawn into the trap of cultural success, or are you going to pursue impact—races that maximize your opportunity to produce positive and lasting impact people can see and feel?

## Finding The Starting Line

The race of life is an amazing invitational. There is an exclusive position on the track only you can fill. You will hear "On your mark" many times over your lifetime, luring you to step up to the wrong starting line—inviting you to invest your scarce time, unique talent and limited resources in exchange for meaningless trophies, possessions and prestige. Races dripping with the potential to rob you of vital and precious opportunities for positive and lasting impact.

Running races rich in impact potential will not be easy. Impactful races will take longer than you think, cost more than you think, be more frustrating than you think and attract more critics than you think. When you accept the invitation to run for impact, you will realize who you were created to become. You will step to the starting line of races rich in impact opportunity. Life-defining races that will leave a lasting and positive impact on the people you love, the teams you lead and the causes that stir your heart.

On your mark - it's time to find the right starting line.

# CHAPTER 3

# Finding the Starting Line: "Choose Well"

*"If you don't know where you are going, you'll end up someplace else."*
—YOGI BERRA, HALL OF FAME CATCHER, N.Y. YANKEES

*"Don't follow the crowd. Let the crowd follow you."*
—MARGARET THATCHER, FORMER PRIME MINISTER OF THE
UNITED KINGDOM

People would walk by us in the park as we watched and ask, "Who is that?" We had no idea at the time. "What is he doing?" would be the next question. We weren't really sure, but it wasn't the familiar recreational jogging we were accustomed to seeing. There was nothing recreational about it. This was two men facing off in a fiercely competitive battle.

Few people knew who he was or what he was doing until a late July evening in 1976. He was best known to his students at Loma Vista Elementary School as Mr. Kardong. His profession was a teacher, but Don Kardong's passion was running—serious running. Don's dream was to run the marathon in the 1976 Olympic Games in Montreal. Part of Kardong's training regimen included sprints around a popular park near my house in Spokane.

The perimeter of Franklin Park measured exactly one mile. The corner of the park, nearest my house, was the starting line. Kardong and his training partner would stand side by side, facing opposite directions. "On your mark, get set, go," and they sprinted off in opposite directions. The starting line was now the finish line, and Don would try to beat his training partner back to the corner.

It was intense! Each lap ran with purpose and conviction. It was fun to see them eye each other's position with about one quarter of a mile to go. You could see them reach down deep and exert every ounce of energy towards the finish. Seemingly completely spent, they would rest for only a few minutes, then put their foot on the starting line and take off again.

Wondering how fast they were running, I would mark their starting time on my watch as they broke from the starting line. To my amazement, they came back into view in nearly four minutes, sprinting full speed as they closed in on the finish. Carefully selected and executed training prepared Don Kardong to win a spot on the 1976 U.S. Olympic Team.

Kardong took his mark for the start of the men's marathon, at the Montreal Olympic Games, on a windy and wet evening, on July 31. Don was well prepared and ran a great race that night. After fighting difficult weather conditions for 25 miles, Don was in position to win an Olympic medal. Kardong's legs began to cramp as they headed down the hill into the stadium tunnel. Only 1.2 miles, little more than one lap around Franklin Park, to the finish line.

As Kardong entered the Olympic Stadium, he was in fourth, place trailing Belgium's Karel Lismont by less than 30 yards. As they eyed the finish line, the crowd in the packed stadium rose to their feet and roared their approval. Both racers were digging deep to finish strong and claim the last medal. Kardong trailed Lismont by only 10 yards with two and a half laps to go.

As they pressed towards the finish line, I pictured Kardong sprinting seemingly effortlessly around Franklin Park mile after mile. I pictured him passing Lismont and capturing an Olympic medal. But in spite of crossing the finish line in a personal best time of 2:11:16, Lismont finished just strides ahead of Kardong, denying him the bronze medal.[1]

> "It's far easier to start something than it is to finish it."
> —Amelia Earhart

## The Critical Choice

Have you ever said, "I wish I had thought of that earlier." Somewhere along life's race everyone has paused for a moment of reflection and acknowledged mistakes and missed opportunities.

Use this time as one of those moments. Now think forward to what it would feel like to come to the end of the marathon of your life and ponder two questions. Who would you want to be in the stadium as you approach the finish line? Has your impact on their lives been significant enough that there is no place they would rather be than cheering your final laps?

Thinking about how you positively impacted these people, imagine entering the stadium for your last few laps. It has been a long journey comprised of many races. You're physically weary, but the sight of the finish line gives you a jolt of energy. The sight of the finish line makes every stride a joyful reminder of your commitment to finish strong.

Setting your sights on the finish line, you don't notice the crowd at first. You're still running to generate positive impact. They have been blessed by your race but don't know what you did to prepare or the sacrifices you had to make along the way. They are largely unaware of what the weather was like along the route, how you felt, if you were hurt, or missed a few milestones along the way. They did not see the challenges you had to overcome or realize how many times you wanted to quit. But they did feel your impact.

As the crowd begins to cheer, you look up and the roar grows louder. Their joy and enthusiasm for your arrival overwhelms the pain pulsating in your feet and the weariness in your legs. As you gaze into the stands, you begin to recognize faces. As you raise your hand and wave to acknowledge their applause, you are overwhelmed with the realization that these are all the people you impacted along the course of your race. Benjamin Disraeli, former Prime Minister of the United Kingdom, said, "The greatest good you can do for another is not just to share your riches but to reveal to him his own."

> "The greatest good you can do for another is not just to share your riches but to reveal to him his own."
> —Benjamin Disraeli

This is what a winning race looks like. Whether this is truly your "final" stadium—death, or one of the many stadiums along your life's journey marking milestones and goals, it will be empty if it does not touch the lives of the people and causes you love. This is impact. This is why you run.

## Life is a Marathon

Many people take credit for saying, "Life is a marathon not a sprint." A statement that changes your perspective from the immediate to the long term, from what may be easy to something painstakingly hard. Barry Magee, an Olympian and the first New Zealander to win an international marathon,[2] said, "Anyone can run 20 miles. It's the next six that count."[3]

The simple marathon of life looks something like this. You don't think too much about your early years, but the idea of becoming a teenager seems important. I am not sure what happens at 13 other than something snatching your body and confusing your judgment. Then it is on to 16 and getting your driver's license. The mere thought of new-found freedom excites you and terrifies your parents and neighbors.

Now the stakes rise, and the race gets more serious. At 18 you get to vote, head off to college, find yourself, and enjoy what sometimes spirals into what you claim to be the greatest four to eight years of your life. You can't wait for milestone marker 21. No one can refuse you service now. You can now claim the full privilege of adulthood while hopefully delaying the responsibility that goes with it. Mistakes you make prior to turning 21 are primarily labeled as silly, maybe even stupid. Mistakes you make after you turn 21 become the shaky early building blocks for your legacy.

Soon you graduate and move back home. Well, it may not be the desired plan, but nearly half of college graduates do it.[4] Finally you find a job you don't like, but eventually land a job you might be able to call a career. You get married, raise the smartest kids ever, abandon your dream to change the world, work hard to cover up the mistakes you told your parents they made, retire and live happily ever after.

Time is linear and marches on unaffected by how you choose to run your race. You add shape and definition to your life based on the races you choose to run and the level of commitment you make to running them. Your races will be filled with ups and downs, periods of acceleration and reflection, wins and losses, and even misdirection. Winning will ultimately be measured in impact—did your races positively change lives?

# How a Single Race Unfolds

### The Story of Life

Every race reflects a cycle that changes with time, decisions and circumstances. A number of years ago, I was introduced to the concept of 'sigmoid curves' by Charles Handy in his book *The Paradox of Change*. Sigmoid curves are the perfect representation of how the individual races of your life unfold and meld together to tell the story of your marathon journey. Handy simply describes the curve this way— "The sigmoid curve sums up the story of life itself. We start slowly, experimentally, and falteringly; we wax and then we wane."[5]

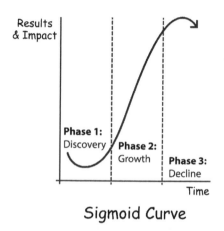

Sigmoid Curve

As you follow the curve, from left to right, it moves through three distinct phases of execution and development. On the vertical axis is the measure of results and impact while the horizontal axis simply represents time

### Three phases of a race

- Phase one: Discovery
- Phase two: Growth
- Phase three: Decline

The shape and duration of the curve is affected by the decisions you make, how you adjust to changing circumstances and conditions, how you respond to feedback, and how you apply your learning and experience along the way.

### *Phase One: Discovery—the early stages of the race*

Have you ever heard the phrase "you don't know what you don't know?" Maybe even scratched your head wondering what it meant? This is the phase of discovery, stepping to the starting line for the first time. You're feeling dumb and happy...or dumb and apprehensive. The technical term would be unconsciously-incompetent. Either way, you don't know what you don't know.

The discovery phase is characterized by excitement and fear. You are attempting to gain competency through the acquisition of knowledge and developing applicable skills. Discovery is the path to figuring out what is going to be required to excel and it means you're going to struggle.

Who doesn't struggle attempting to learn new things and working on your own for the first time? Even simple things required a phase of discovery. From making your bed, to riding your bike or doing chores around the house, you had to experience doing them for yourself before you achieved a degree of proficiency. With some practice and coaching you mastered them—maybe with the exception of making beds for some people.

The struggles associated with the discovery phase rise with complexity. Performance and results might even decline, which heighten challenges, frustrations and disappointments. With progress stalled, the motivation that drove you toward future rewards gets pushed aside. This is when you quit, businesses fail and ambition dies.

I remember watching a talented young man taking golf lessons. Already a proficient player, his coach made a change that was critical to him becoming an elite player. After the coach told the young man why he needed to make the change, showed him the change, and demonstrated it, the coach said, "Be patient! You are going to get worse before you get better. But better will improve your game significantly over where it is today."

> "When we make progress quickly, it feeds our emotions. Then, when there's a period a waiting or we hit a plateau, we find out how committed we really are and whether we're going to see things through to the finish or quit."
> —Joyce Meyer

### *Winners never quit and quitters never win unless...*

Putting your foot on the mark to start a new race will always bring some risk. I loved the sound of the piano enough to write down "Learn to play the piano" on a dream list I constructed years ago. My wife set the pursuit of this dream in motion by giving me a keyboard for Christmas and making arrangements for me to take some lessons.

I knew I was dumb and happy heading to my first lesson, and it wouldn't take long for my teacher to agree. As we got acquainted, she asked me some questions to measure my level of musical knowledge. I had never played an instrument, but based on singing in school choir, I knew how to read a bit of music. She immediately plugged me into the discovery phase of the journey. I was dumb and happy—visions of Handel playing through my head. She had nightmares of Chopsticks.

She laid out the discovery phase step by step. We went through the lesson books, spent some time getting familiar with the keyboard, and laying out my practice assignments. I practiced diligently, completed my assignments, and tried to not let anything conflict with our scheduled lesson time. After a few months, I thought I was gaining some traction and progressing nicely through the discovery phase, at least until my teacher asked me this question, "Mr. Akers, are you practicing?"

My first thought before responding was, "Are you kidding? You must not be listening attentively. My wife thinks I am doing great." I kept my indignant disappointment to myself and replied, "Absolutely. I am practicing and following the lesson plan you have laid out."

I was surprised, in a state of disbelief, and one comment away from being reduced to feeling like a first grader. "Then I must conclude that you do not have any musical talent, and you should seriously consider whether you want to continue taking lessons," she replied. I can laugh about this now, but this was not the feedback I was expecting. I am not a quitter—I wanted to play the piano! I wanted to be at a family gathering and sit down and rock that piano like Harry Connick Jr..

This is not a story of victory where I tell you I broke through my lack of talent and the crushing feedback from a teacher. I did what every smart, middle-aged piano student, who lacked musical talent would do—I quit!

Not all was lost. I did get a good story to explain what happens in the discovery phase of running a new race. If you were expecting winners never quit and quitters never win, we'll save that for later.

The discovery phase will always be defined by struggle, learning and new beginnings. Discovery is not a playground reserved exclusively for the young. Discovery rises up to greet anyone who starts a new race regardless of age, energy, ambition or experience. Your intellectual and emotional age is largely a reflection of how you respond to the struggles and challenges presented by the new beginnings of discovery.

### Phase Two: Growth—finding your way to impact

Anything worth doing is worth doing poorly until you learn to do it well. Welcome to the growth phase or the phase of conscious-competency. You are developing the habits and traits of performance excellence, but you have to think about them while you are performing. You have not reached a level of sustained competency, but you are committed to figuring it out.

This is where I would've learned how to play Pachelbel's *Canon*. This is where the race picks up speed and momentum, and the curve begins to rise sharply. The "S" shape in the curve begins to climb and elongate. You begin applying the new learning, knowledge and feedback acquired in the discovery phase. You begin to produce some positive results, confidence grows, and signs of mastery appear.

The growth phase is where you gain command of school, careers take off, businesses expand, and relationships grow and mature. It is a time of rising expectations and expanding capabilities. The race is exciting and fun, and with new growth comes increasing opportunity for impact. You are now in the performance zone where you have melded your skills, knowledge, and understanding into instinctive and habitual behavior and action. This is the point where I would've been ready for a recital.

### Phase Three: Decline, it's time to start a new race.

Every race has a finish line. Paulo Coelho, acclaimed best-selling author of *The Alchemist*, wrote, "It is always important to know when something has reached its end. Closing circles, shutting doors, finishing chapters, it doesn't matter what we call it; what matters is to leave in the past those moments in life that are over."[6]

This is the decline phase of a race. Some declines are gradual—a point where performance peaks, contribution flattens, interest shifts or passion is lost. Decline is painful for two reasons. First, you are leaving something both familiar and successful. Second, you hate the struggle associated with discovery and dread the thought of starting over. It is hard to leave in the past those races that are over—especially if you were enjoying some success. No one likes to close the door on past success. As strange as it may sound you may even cling to failings.

Gradual decline may be hard to detect, but some declines are sudden and emotional. They are unexpected, unplanned, and they are going to happen. The loss of a loved one, losing a job, facing a difficult health situation, or suffering a significant financial loss bring an abrupt end to a race. Decline is difficult but it does not have to define the end.

## Building the Second Curve

Yes, our biological decline is inevitable—you will come to the end of your race. But this marathon we call life is not a single curve but a series of curves. "A good life is probably a succession of second curves, started before the first curve fades."[7]

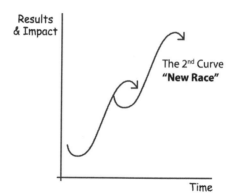

Your challenge, regardless of what brings you to the finish line of a race, is to step to the starting line of a new race before entering decline. The vision to launch second curves comes from redirecting your talent, resources and passion towards new impact-rich opportunities.

Following the 1976 Olympics, Don Kardong continued to compete on the international racing stage. But he did not appear in another Olympic games. Before he peaked as an elite athlete, he started new races. His

Olympic appearance sparked a running craze in Spokane. Capitalizing on his celebrity and expertise, Don opened a running store called "The Human Race" and founded Bloomsday, one of the largest road races in America.[8]

Every race travels through this cycle of discovery, growth and decline. The principal reason you do not transition well from the finish of one race to the start line of a new race is failing to pay attention to the signs along the way that indicate the peak of the curve is approaching and heading into decline.

### Milestone Markers and What Do They Mean?

Do you pay attention to street signs and milestone markers on routes you travel frequently? Does anyone? Of course not. Familiarity is synonymous with autopilot. I am a landmark driver so the only way to get my attention when I am driving on a familiar route is to change a significant landmark. However, travel into unfamiliar territory and the game changes.

Do you know the feelings of anticipation and anxiety you get when you are driving to an unfamiliar destination? My family and I landed in Boston on our way to Cape Cod. It was my wife's first trip to Boston. I sensed her uneasiness as we left the rental car lot. As we pulled away, she asked me if I knew where I was going. I had been to Boston a number of times and said, "As long as we pass the guy selling coffee from a jet pack, at the exit of the airport, I think I know where I am going."

Road markers and signage help assure you're on the right road, making the right turns, progressing as planned, and maybe even driving the right speed. The milestone markers along the curve of your race are personal inflection points. These are the life events and experiences that must command your attention. Personal inflection points help you to stay on track and point to changing conditions that could affect your race.

As the curve of a race eventually peaks out and heads towards decline, you will see three important milestone markers. These markers indicate you are reaching the summit and it is time to start a new race (new curve) before you head into decline.

1. Seasons of life milestones—markers that appear as part of the natural progression of life.

2. Change milestones—markers created when the rate of change is greater than our ability to adapt.
3. Warning milestones—markers that present themselves based on energy, interest or commitment interfering with our ability to run the race.

### Milestone Marker #1: Seasons of life

Who isn't in a rush to grow up when we are young? But then as we grow older, we make every attempt to reclaim our youth. At every stage of my life I have experienced moments where I shook my head wondering how I arrived at this point in my life so quickly. If you haven't had this experience, you will. I now look at my hands and know seasons have come and gone because somewhere along the course of this journey my hands began to look like my dad's.

The seasons of life are beyond your control, never asking you if you want to participate. But they beg your engagement. The seasons of life will unfold with unpredictable predictability, bringing with them periods of unending joy, incredible victory, moments of solitude and unwelcome pain. Changing seasons are marked by graduations, new relationships, marriage, the birth of a child or grandchild, promotions, new jobs, planned retirement or launching a business. They are also marked by the reality of sudden and unexpected loss that can instantaneously change your roles and responsibilities.

> "There is a time for everything, and a season for activity under heaven."
> —Solomon

While seasons change without permission, they are held together by the fact that in every season and circumstance you will be presented with opportunities for incredible impact. Solomon said, "There is a time for everything, and a season for activity under heaven."

Acknowledging and enjoying your current season of life is a choice—a critical choice. The harvest in every season is a reflection of the seeds you plant and nurture. What you have to understand and embrace is that seasons pass. You don't get to go back and relive your youth, recapture romance or enjoy being a mom or dad. Nor do you get to go back and reverse decisions that yielded fleeting joy in favor of saving, investing and creating a foundation for your future.

Each season stands on its own and will present you with races you may not feel like running. But the harvest of the season cannot be reaped with good intentions—it will require sacrifice, discipline and hard work. Seasons change—it is up to you to decide how you will run the race.

### Milestone Marker #2: Change

"There is nothing permanent except change." A contemporary theme uttered 2,500 years ago by Heraclitus, the Greek philosopher. No one is immune from change as it constantly exerts itself upon the direction and trajectory of your race. The change milestone appears when the rate of change that drives performance requirements outstrips your base of knowledge, effort, abilities, or commitment. With the rapid acceleration in the rate of change, be aware that the ascent of the growth curve peaks more quickly.

Knowing change is constant does not make it easy to recognize its infringement upon the progress of your race. Sometimes the strength of your expectations can blind you to impending change. A talented IT professional came to me trying to understand how to navigate some unexpected changes. He had risen to a prominent role in his company based on his technical competence and leadership. After a series of organizational changes and promotions, Robert did not get a promotion he expected. While this was disappointing, what was of greater concern was being told his lack of a college degree could keep him from being considered for future promotions.

This is what a change milestone marker looks like. Robert can hope that his lack of a degree will not hold him back or that he can fill in the gap by completing his degree. Change milestones alert you to make course corrections. Leo Tolstoy wrote, "Everyone thinks of changing the world, but no one thinks of changing himself."

Ignoring markers that alert you to change present a real danger. Just because you don't acknowledge or accept the advance of change does not mean your race won't be profoundly altered. Change milestones are there to alert you to shift careers, question whether a passion could be converted to a vocation, expect the possibility of an unplanned retirement, changing health or an unraveling financial foundation.

Ignoring or avoiding change breeds routine and complacency that will blindside you. Change speeds your race up and can quickly and unexpectedly bring your race to its peak and push you into decline. The danger of being pushed into decline is that it is much steeper, more pronounced and happens faster than you think—especially the bigger the change milestone is.


### Milestone Marker #3: Warnings

What would you do if the "check engine" light came on in your car while you were driving? What does that light really mean anyway? Is it a real warning signal that requires attention? Maybe it has happened to you. How did you respond? How should you respond?

When the check engine light came on in my niece's car for the first time she ignored it. Why? Because it went off. She ignored it for the second time, well, because it went off again. The third time it came on it stayed on. But given it had already gone off twice, in her experience, it would eventually turn off again. So, she ignored it. Then a friend told her that she thought her car was smoking. A thorough check of the engine revealed that a small leak had drained nearly all of the engine oil, nearly causing the engine to seize up.

You have a personal check engine light tied to your energy, interest and commitment. When any of these three vital race fluids wane, the light should illuminate, alerting you to the potential of a problem. The subtle and changing nature of these vital race fluids can make it difficult to recognize this milestone marker without some help and encouragement.

This milestone marker is critical to races where relationships are at stake. These are the races that touch your families, the people you lead and the teams you play on. The stakes are high, and the long-term impact cautionary. Without energy, interest and commitment, relationships fail, careers stall, health fades and dreams die. Races get interrupted by illness, addiction, affairs, conflicting ambition and changing agendas when you ignore your personal "check engine" light.

Much of the joy you get from running a race is realized just before reaching the peak. It is a time of great familiarity so it also means you are less likely to see or acknowledge the mile-stone markers as you approach the summit. Every race you run will eventually need a second curve. Impact grows and expands out your ability to transition from one race to another. The best time to invest in a new curve is on the way up. The best time to execute the future is before it arrives.

> **Impact grows and expands out your ability to transition from one race to another.**

## Choose Well!

Impact grows and multiplies with the creation of second curves (new races). Your ability to sustain and extend impact is enriched by adopting the mindset that you are always closer to the peak of a race than you think. Lasting impact cannot be secured in a single race. It is a series of races that push you to find new starting lines—to ask, "What's next?"

The Walt Disney Company has built a generation of advertising and promotion around its "What's Next?" campaign. After Phil Simms quarterbacked the New York Giants to victory in Super Bowl XXI over the Denver Broncos, they asked him, "Phil Simms, you've just won the Super Bowl. What are you going to do next?" He shouted out, "I'm going to Disney World!"[9] A phrase now associated with one of the greatest advertising campaigns in history and a part of our pop lexicon, "What's next?" should become part of your race plan for creating sustained impact.

Imagine you have come to the end of an important race. You begin to think about the people you have touched, and the results achieved. The story of your race's impact is being projected on the giant stadium video board with the iconic song *When You Wish Upon A Star* from *Pinocchio* playing in the background. The video comes to an end and fades to the words, "What's next?" This is the moment, with images of fireworks exploding over Cinderella's Castle at Disney World, to commit to embarking on a new race.

> "Every moment is a golden one for him who has the vision to recognize it as such."
> —Henry Miller

The Greek philosopher Zeno wrote, "If a traveler goes halfway to his destination each day he can never reach his final destination since there's always another half way to go." Impact is embracing the next race. Impact is looking for the second curve and pushing yourself through the fear, uncertainty and discomfort of starting anew. The path of the race never changes—discovery, growth and decline. What changes is which races you choose to run, how you choose to run them and your level of commitment to positively impact the people you love, the teams you lead and the causes that stir your heart.

# CHAPTER 4

# Be Rich Towards What Counts: "Real Wealth Starts with a Question"

*"The two most important days in your life are the day you were born and the day you find out why."*
—MARK TWAIN

*Never confuse activity for significance and impact. Can we agree that meaning doesn't come from what we have to do to survive but from what we do that adds value to the lives of others?*
—MATTHEW BARNETT, THE CAUSE WITHIN YOU

I didn't know a soul when I walked into the room. I scanned the crowded room looking for a table with an empty seat. Maneuvering through the maze of tables I began to feel a bit uneasy as people were already deeply engaged in conversation. As my thoughts tugged me towards escaping my uneasiness by opting for room service, I was met with a smile sitting next to an empty seat.

I was greeted with a warm "Hey," wrapped in a charming southern accent. As I sat down, Josh's and Aly's warmth and energy quickly overwhelmed my uneasiness. I had no idea what the evening held in store, but they had me at "Hey." I quickly became intrigued by their hope and curiously asked, "Tell me your story." You never know where this simple question will lead.

Tonight it opened the door to the completely unexpected. Josh narrated the story while Aly filled in the missing pieces and sprinkled it with understated emotion. Their story started when they were kids. But, looking at them, they were still kids but seemingly far from being newlyweds.

Josh caught Aly's attention when she was a freshman in high school, but he failed to capture her heart the first time around. When a second opportunity presented itself, he not only captured her heart...he captured her hand in marriage. They liked the imagery of an older man sweeping a younger woman off her feet, but at 21 and 19 they were both young. They grew up together, learned about love together, and while they were figuring out marriage together, a fateful twist of life would change them forever.

What do you do when an unwanted and unwelcome villain enters your fairytale? Josh shared these words with Aly on their wedding day, "I promise to protect you, lead you, and care for you until the last breath I take. I want to care for you when everything is great and when life throws us struggles that make our world shake."[1] Just five short years was all it would take for everything great to begin to shake—Aly was diagnosed with breast cancer.

Over a period of three-and-a-half years, Aly endured a bilateral mastectomy, chemotherapy, radiation and four major surgeries. As they are describing the battles and emotions of fighting cancer, I hurriedly tried to piece the timeline together. I suddenly realize this beautiful and vibrant young lady was just now entering the recovery phase of this battle for her life. Josh's and Aly's story wasn't something from the distant past. They were racing for Aly's life and their dreams in the moment.

When the world shakes, the race changes for most of us. You turn your attention away from the future and entrench yourself in a battle for daily survival. The uncertainty of shaking urgently pushes you to grasp for anything resembling comfort and stability.

At this point I am expecting to hear Josh and Aly describe what this fight looks like. Instead, Aly tells me she is nearing the completion of her doctorate degree in Family and Marriage Counseling. I can't help but think, "Why?" How do you set your sights on the future in the face of grave uncertainty? Josh and Aly offered great insight—be rich towards what counts. What counted was their marriage, their faith and their family. Who could have imagined that a smile, an empty chair and a simple question would open the door to such great wisdom.

On the last day of the conference Josh asked me if I would consider mentoring him. I think he had it turned around. Maybe he should be mentoring me. This was a young man who had it together—loving parents, grounded male role models, caring friends, focused ambition and an incredible wife.

What could I possibly offer Josh? He had run races that exposed him to the trap of cultural success. Along the course of his young race, he had recognized and worked through more challenges and milestone markers than most of us deal with in a lifetime. Just as iron sharpens iron, he had forged a clear sense of what it meant to be rich out of crushing circumstances.

Authenticity and transparency are like magnets that draw you in. Josh modestly acknowledged his strengths and vulnerably pointed out his weaknesses and flaws. Unlike me, he was comfortable telling people about his mistakes and failings. I was intrigued by how honestly he talked about his fears, the struggles he and Aly had faced together, and how it shaped his perspective and attitude. I admired his desire to become the man God created him to be. I wasn't sure what I had to offer, but I couldn't say no.

Leading up to our first call, I thought about where to begin. Now back home in Louisiana, when Josh answered the phone, his southern accent was more distinct and shone even brighter. Just listening to him talk brought a smile to my face. As Josh expressed his desire to gain clarity about his priorities, I asked him what he thought it meant to be rich towards what counts.

I am not sure what I expected Josh to say. What was tugging on his heart was fueling an aerobic workout in his mind. Thinking out loud, he bounced around the question as he worked to gain clarity. Then Josh paused for a moment and said, "I think being rich towards what counts means would I still be content if all my possessions went away."

> Being rich towards what counts means would I still be content if all my possessions went away.

It wasn't the answer I was expecting. Were you? What does it mean to be rich towards what counts? Your answer to this question is one of the keys to running a race filled with lasting and meaningful impact.

## Get Specific

On your marks! The race to impact, to becoming who you were created to be, begins with being rich towards what counts. Lily Tomlin is a celebrated comic and actress. Deflecting praise for her accomplishments, she said, "I always wanted to be somebody. I wish I would have been more specific." You are going to be somebody regardless of what you do. Why not be specific and intentional? Why shouldn't you run a race dedicated to changing lives—creating lasting and meaningful impact?

Who do you need to become to raise your impact? I was helping a young man get specific. We started with building a plan to launch his career. As we reviewed his plan, I pressed him to be more specific. Thinking his answers were clear, concise and specific, he asked, "Why do you keep emphasizing clarity?" "Because," I replied, "clarity pushes randomness, confusion and hesitancy to the sideline. Clarity eliminates distractions and focuses your thoughts and actions on what you have identified as being important. Clarity infuses you with persistent determination."

### Life must be lived forwards

> "Life can only be understood backwards; but it must be lived forwards."
> —Soren Kierkegaard

Soren Kierkegaard, the incomparable Danish philosopher and theologian, wrote, "Life can only be understood backwards; but it must be lived forwards." Over the course of my business career I sent thousands of birthday cards. One of my favorite things to write was, "Gather up all of your life's experiences and invest them in filling your new year of age with joy and impact." You are at your best when you are effectively using your experiences to live forwards.

While your life is always moving forward, it does not mean you are living forward. "Time and tide wait for no man"[2] is a phrase predating modern English. With its earliest known record being in the year 1225, man has long understood that none of us are capable of stopping the march of time.

Living forward means fully investing yourself in finishing strong—to run a victorious race, an impactful race. The most glorious finish line resides at the intersection of your passions and the races rich with potential for impact. It is where your vision is clear and strong enough to push aside the nonimportant and nonessential. Winning the race means being rich towards what truly counts.

## Discovering Your Riches

What's your story? Pause for a moment and think about it for a moment. If you had 30 seconds to summarize your current story, what picture would you paint? Would it place you on a journey towards lasting and sustainable impact? Your best story will be produced by directing your time, talent and resources in pursuit of being rich towards what is most important to you.

*The Number* by Lee Eisenberg is an intriguing exploration of how and why people arrive at "the number"—the financial resources they believe will assure life-long financial security. Lee interviewed people from all walks of life and sought the expertise and experience of wealth managers, financial experts and life coaches. He suggests you have a number that defines the unknown and elusive point where your net worth intersects with your self-worth.

After a thorough and thoughtful review, Eisenberg concludes, "A financial plan without a meaning plan leads straight to the thudding realization that—duh—all the money in the world doesn't buy happiness."[3]

Happiness requires a meaning plan—a plan scripted around running races capable of delivering meaningful and lasting impact. It is a plan that can only evolve from a foundational definition of success capable of standing the test of time, guiding you through all of the milestone warnings, and supporting you in all seasons of life.

### *Defining real success?*

I have been testing and massaging my definition of success for as long as I can remember. When I am speaking, I will preface sharing this definition of success by saying it is universal. If you are looking for skeptics, just claim something is universal. Suggest one-size-fits-all for success, and you can be certain to pique people's interest, not out of real interest in learning, but in anticipation of igniting a debate by suggesting you are wrong.

> "Success is the identification of your most important roles, values, and goals, and living your personal and professional life in alignment with your chosen roles, values, and goals."

So in the interest of real learning and welcoming disagreement and debate, here is my universal, one-size-fits-all definition of success: "Success is the identification of your most important roles, values, and goals, and living your personal and professional life in alignment with your chosen roles, values, and goals."

As you think about this definition, challenge the tenets of the definition, and consider its personal nature. People (almost unanimously) conclude it is in fact universal.

I continue to find that...regardless of your age, gender, marital status, economic standing, professional ascent or any other criteria...you can think of this definition of success as being applicable because it focuses you on being rich towards what counts. Roles, values and goals set the course for your race. They focus your time, talent and resources on being rich towards what counts—being rich towards the people and causes you want to positively impact.

### It's one thing

In the movie City Slickers, actor Billy Crystal plays the character Mitch Robbins, a big-city radio ads salesman who is having a mid-life crisis. He and his friends Phil Berquist (Daniel Stern) and Ed Furillo (Bruno Kirby) are in the midst of what they perceive to be a personal crisis. They are finding out that the pursuit of cultural success is not producing the sense of joy and accomplishment they imagined.

Mitch's wife throws him a 39th birthday party. Huddled in the kitchen discussing the state of their lives, Mitch, Phil and Ed conclude that they need to escape and create some excitement. Perhaps confirming that they are not thinking clearly, they decide there could be nothing more exciting than a two-week trip to drive cattle from New Mexico to Colorado.

What starts as an escape from reality turns into a search for real success. Mitch finds himself befriended by Curly Washburn (Jack Palance).

Curly is a worldly, wise, tough-as-nails trail boss. Out on the trail Mitch rides up alongside Curly and begins to lament his personal crisis. Believing Curly to be the curator of great wisdom Mitch asks him, "What is the meaning of life?"

Curly doesn't hesitate for a moment. He looks at Mitch and holds up one finger. Mitch begins to laugh, disbelieving this could be the answer. Chuckling while looking at Curly's finger, Mitch asks, "What does that mean?" Without even a hint of a smile, Curly replies, "It's the one thing that is for you to figure out."

As their wild adventure unfolds, they begin to figure out that the "one thing" is focusing their time and attention on being rich towards what counts. Mitch, Phil and Ed return to New York and recommit themselves to their families. They no longer see their work as a means of defining success but as a platform to support the most important people in their lives.

Being rich towards what counts requires you to think *who* first. Life's marathon is a long and arduous journey filled with distractions capable of incapacitating your impact. Maximizing your impact requires thoughtful contemplation—to plan, prepare and focus on the people and causes touched by the most important roles in your life. Most people allow their race to unfold by chance and accident.

Being rich towards what counts requires you to be intentional about how you are going to run your race. By clearly defining success, starting with your most important roles, you will have defined the finish line for your race.

## You Will Never Be the Same

While Albert Einstein was teaching at the Institute for Advanced Study in Princeton, he asked his teaching assistants to administer an upcoming test. Upon reviewing the test, the assistant noticed that it was the same test the students took the previous semester. Hesitantly, the assistant brought the mistake to Einstein's attention. The unflappable professor looked at his young assistant and said, "Yes, you are correct. It is the same exam." Taken aback by the professor's answer, the assistant pressed, "But how can you give them the same test they just took?" Einstein smiled and replied, "Simply because the answers have changed."[4]

> Your mind once challenged with a question never retreats to its previous state.

Questions set your mind in motion. Your mind once challenged with a question never retreats to its previous state. What do you think the students in Einstein's class thought when they saw the exam? Exactly... these are the same questions as the last exam. Wouldn't you like to know how many students thought the answers were different? It is so easy to dismiss a question when you think you've already answered it.

But, what if finding new answers to old questions held the key to helping you sustain impact over the course of your race? What if taking the same exam, over and over, guided you towards selecting, running and finishing races that you would have missed otherwise? It is a simple two-question exam sure to keep your race focused on being rich towards what counts.

### 1. *Who do you want to be remembered by?*

This is not a question that screams of urgency early in life. Thinking about who you want to be remembered by tends to flow from changes in life that come with added responsibility rather than intentional and deliberate thought. This became very clear to me during a college internship with Northwestern Mutual Life Insurance Company. Can you imagine selling life insurance to college students? Yes, college students, whose financial priorities were tuition, books, rent, beer and pizza. And, for some, it was not even in that order.

One day, the light came on. I was talking to a friend who was in ROTC and dreamed of being a pilot. Life insurance underwriting is very specific about excluding coverage for past engagement in risky activities—including flying. I knew Scott had a girlfriend he was planning to marry after graduating. When I asked Scott about life insurance, he laughed like nearly everyone else. Then I asked him about his plans for flying and family. As soon as he thought about who he wanted to be remembered by, my question about life insurance could no longer be excused as laughable.

Casual questions generate simple conversation. Important questions force thinking at levels that create discomfort. There is nothing casual about identifying who you want to be remembered by. I was working with a talented young lady who was struggling to get her career launched. What do struggling college graduates think they should do next? Right—go to graduate school and avoid putting a foot into the real world! When I asked her who she wanted to be remembered by, she quickly pushed back, "I don't understand what this has to do with finding a job."

She was right. It had nothing to do with finding a job. Finding a job is easy and wasn't the objective. The challenge was to create a life that allowed her to be rich towards what she valued most. I pressed her for an answer and she continued to push back. So I asked her, "Do you know anyone who has regrets about their life?" It did not take her long to begin sharing stories of regret. In mid-sentence, as she spoke about other people's regrets, she had an "ah-ha" moment.

She realized that identifying who she most wanted to be remembered by allowed her to work backwards from what she wanted most. Knowing who she wanted to be remembered most by would lead her to select races aligned with the people, relationships and causes she loved and valued most.

Whether you are just getting started, in the middle of life's complexities or planning your transition to post-career pursuits, what matters is being intentional about where you are going from here. You can never make up for lost time, but you can always make the best of your time going forward. Answering the question "Who do you want to be remembered by?" identifies who you want to be in the stadium when you cross the finish line of important races. It clarifies your most important roles. Your commitment to excellence in these roles creates impact opportunities. Everything you want to accomplish will be started, extended and sustained through relationships.

### 2. *What do you want to be remembered for?*

Impact is striving to change a life forever. The change event, experience or contribution that creates impact is the answer to the second question, "What do you want to be remembered for?" This is the impact question. What are you going to do to impact the people you love, the teams you lead and the causes that stir your heart?

> **If you want to be disappointed by your future, don't think about it.**

This is a strategic question. Its very nature is futuristic and visionary. It challenges you to think beyond the immediacy and practicality of what is necessary today. Peter Drucker said, "If you want to predict the future, create it"— the corollary being that if you want to be disappointed by your future, don't think about it. The reason you are surprised by a future you did not expect is that you don't spend enough time thinking about where you want to end up.

Jim Rohn, best selling author and speaker, once said, "If you don't design your own life plan, chances are you'll fall into someone else's plan. And guess what they have planned for you? Not much." Creating impact that changes a life forever can only be achieved by delivering what you want to be remembered for to the people you want to be remembered by.

## What Rich Looks Like

When you intentionally decide to run races that support the most important roles in your life, you will be instantly and profoundly changed. When you study people who are running a successful race, you routinely see support from someone who was fully committed to their success. Behind every successful leader, coach, teacher, manager or friend is someone who was deeply and passionately committed to his or her health, development and well-being. In the case of Andy Grove, it was his parents.

Andy Grove was the long-time CEO of Intel Corporation. Under Grove's leadership, Intel rose to become one of the world's most successful and admired companies. Business historians have suggested his accomplishments "merit a place alongside the great business leaders of the 20th century,"[5] and *Time Magazine* named him its "Man of the Year" in 1997. Grove's achievements are a reflection of his commitment to his role as a husband, father, son, leader, author, and friend.

Grove chronicled his early life in his autobiography, *Swimming Across*. If it were not for the commitment of his mom and dad to their roles as parents, we may have never heard of Andy Grove. In 1944, when Grove was eight, the Nazis occupied his homeland of Hungary. During the occupation, the Nazis deported nearly 500,000 Jews to concentration camps. During this time, his father was shipped off to a labor camp while he and his mother sought shelter and safety in the homes of friends.

In 1956, Andy's parents and aunt encouraged Andy to escape the country during the Hungarian Revolution. There were only two problems according to Andy—"I didn't know how to do it, and I was scared." They put a plan together, and here is how Andy described his departure:

"We said goodbye at the corner as if it were any normal morning. We didn't dare make a big production of it; it would not have been a good idea to suggest that I was doing anything out of the ordinary. We parted; then I stopped in my tracks. I had automatically put the key to our apartment in my pocket. Now I fished it out, turned around, and ran after my parents. I handed it to my mother and said awkwardly 'I probably won't need this anymore.' My mother nodded. She looked as if she wanted to say something, but she didn't speak. I saw that there were tears in her eyes."[6]

The tears communicated her love. It was out of love that she fulfilled her commitment as a mother to protect her son. When Andy Grove arrived in the United States, in 1957, he had already finished a number of important races that would've discouraged and defeated most people. Andy arrived in New York City aboard the *General W. G. Haan* armed with some broken English, healthy ambition and a hopeful attitude.

Everything of worldly value had been taken from him, but he was content with the opportunity to be called to the starting line, to run a new race. Andy Grove's incredible race of impact was first made possible by parents who were fully committed to their roles. Andy Grove's impact on his marriage, family and business is a reflection of knowing who he wanted to be remembered by and what he wanted to be remembered for. Andy Grove understood the value and importance of being rich towards what counts.

Mitch asked Curly, "What is the meaning of life?" Curly was right. It is one thing—identifying your most important roles, values and goals and living your personal and professional life in alignment with your chosen roles, values and goals.

This is where we begin being rich towards what matters to you. It is a point of dramatic empowerment because when you hear "On your mark!" you will be crystal clear about the roles you must remain committed to in order to exhaust your time, talent and resources towards positively impacting the people you love, the teams you lead and the causes that stir your hearts.

# CHAPTER 5

# Don't Be Disappointed: "You've Got to Get This Right"

*"He is no fool who gives up what he cannot keep to gain what he cannot lose."*
—*JIM ELLIOT*

*"Action expresses priorities."*
—*MAHATMA GANDHI*

I heard it before, but I obviously wasn't paying attention. It wasn't the first time someone shared invaluable wisdom with me and I missed it. Ironic how hindsight always leaves you wondering how it's possible to miss invaluable counsel. You are certainly free to learn important lessons on your own, but it is so much wiser to draw upon the experience of others.

I was determined that this time would be different. Now I coveted Larry's wisdom and advice. His reputation was legendary and for good reason. Larry was a trusted advisor to many successful business leaders inside and outside of our company. Over the course of his career he produced a celebrated track record of performance. But, beyond his business acumen, there was something unique and special about Larry that was hard to put your finger on.

In the 1970's E. F. Hutton was an iconic stock brokerage brand built upon a famous and often-quoted tag line. Its commercials would picture two people, in a crowded venue buzzing with conversation and activity, having an attentive conversation about investing. After the first person shared his broker's investment opinion, he would look at his friend and ask, "What does your broker think?" He'd reply, "Well, my broker is E. F. Hutton. And E. F. Hutton says..." At this point everyone stops what they are doing and leans in to listen. The picture fades to the E. F. Hutton logo and you hear, "When E. F. Hutton talks, people listen."[1] Larry was like E. F. Hutton. When Larry spoke, people listened.

You expected to scratch out notes and tuck them away for future reference when Larry was around. Larry possessed a keen sense for identifying and focusing on what was important—listening, assessing and evaluating before he'd cut through the clutter to put a spot light on what was truly important.

Larry's intellect was intimidating. But wrapped inside a warm and engaging personality he had a way of making you feel important. Warmth and wisdom were just what I needed, so I was thrilled when Larry accepted an invitation to attend a meeting I was hosting. As the date of our meeting approached, I was fully invested in the complexity of running a lot of different races—husband, young father and career builder.

If you have ever felt tugged in a variety of different directions you know exactly what I am talking about. As a husband and father, I was trying to accelerate and struggling not to let my career aspirations overwhelm my attention. We had moved a couple times as a family and my current responsibilities had me on the road traveling nearly every week. I had done a good job of training my boys as to why I worked so hard. Just ask them why and they would quickly say, "Because Dad loves us." I did love them, and while hearing them say "Because Dad loves us" made me feel good, it did not mask the fact that I had more work to do as a husband and a father.

> "Ambition is like love, impatient both of delays and rivals."
> —Sir John Denham

Ambition is a powerful force that pulls you towards the finish line. Sir John Denham, a 16th century writer and poet, said, "Ambition is like love, impatient both of delays and rivals." This brewing impatience fuels desire and pushes you to run right by important milestone markers and exits—even push you off your desired course. In the absence of sound counsel, unbridled ambition leads you towards a finish line draped with disappointment. It was a good time to talk to Larry.

Our business meeting kicked off over dinner. I got there early to welcome everyone when they arrived. One by one people filed in but no sign of Larry. When he finally walked in, he immediately came over to thank me for the invitation. I was thrilled and relieved to see him. He extended his hand. As I reached for his, he wrapped both hands around my right hand and offered up a smile that affirmed our friendship. You know that feeling of being in the presence of a genuine friend? This was one of those moments.

## Making the Complex Simple

The next day after morning meetings, Larry rode with me to lunch. On our 15-minute ride to the restaurant, Larry wasted no time engaging me in a dialogue about my life. He knew I was being considered for a new opportunity and understood future promotions would require me to move my family.

In disarming fashion Larry asked a few questions seeking clarity and understanding. After listening to me outline all the pro's and con's for various moves in my career, Larry was about to take my complex explanation and make it incredibly simple. He was going to share wisdom and advice that is essential to running an impactful race and crossing the right finish line.

I know he had said it to me before, but this time would be different. I was ready to hear it. "Jim," Larry began, "You can climb as high as you want to climb in your career. You could be CEO of this company." He then paused. I know Larry did not want me to focus on what he thought I could achieve in my career or allow me to be distracted by his praise or affirmation. Drawing my attention out of the corner office and back to him he simply said, "Remember, if you put your family first, you will never be disappointed."

That was it! There was nothing more to say. Ambition, complexity and opportunity simplified. Your life is made up of many different roles. Life can be messy but only one role can be number one. It had to be similar to what happened to Mitch on the cattle drive with Curly—it's one thing!

Creating and delivering impact requires you to identify and choose the one role amongst what looks like many equals to guide and shape your race. The only way to create impact that positively changes and improves lives is to fully understand what you are trying to create. It's not really possible to deliver lasting and meaningful impact without a clear understanding and commitment to your most important role.

You might think it bold to place so much importance on identifying your number one role. But just take a moment and think about the fact that you have a finite amount of time, talent and resources. By concentrating on what stirs your heart and commands your attention, you give yourself the best opportunity to maximize your race's impact. The goal is not to run through the motions of the race but to break the tape knowing you ran an intentional, purposeful and meaningful race.

## Your View of the World

This wheel represents all the roles you play in your life. Each spoke represents a specific role.

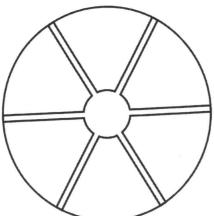

### Picturing Your Life Roles
(The role you place in the center
influences every role in your life.)

Whether by conscious choice or default, the role you place in the center of the wheel ultimately influences and shapes all of your decisions. The quality and impact of your race will ultimately reflect where the sum of where your decisions take you. You make decisions every day. Every decision you make is determined by your priorities. The role you place in the center becomes the lens through which you'll decide which races you'll run and how you'll run them. The role in the center shapes your view of the world.

One of my favorite movies is *Ferris Bueller's Day Off*. Ferris (Matthew Broderick), his girlfriend Sloane Peterson (Mia Sara) and best friend Cameron Frye (Alan Ruck) decide to skip school and spend the day exploring the sites, sounds and cuisine of downtown Chicago. Ferris arrives at Cameron's house and coaxes his reluctant friend into taking his father's prized 1961 Ferrari 250 GT California Spider convertible out for their day of high jinx.

> **Whether by conscious choice or default, the role you place in the center of the wheel ultimately influences and shapes all of your decisions.**

Sitting in the back seat, Cameron begins to verbalize all the things he thinks his dad is going to do to him when his dad discovers he took the car. While Cameron imaginatively visualizes the wrath of his father, all Ferris can see is the three of them having the time of their lives. They pull the Ferrari into a parking garage where they are enthusiastically greeted by two suspect-looking valets. Not to fear, Ferris hands them a five-dollar bill to insure the car's safety.

While Ferris, Cameron and Sloane enjoy a lively tour of every landmark in the city of Chicago, the valets seize the opportunity to take the Ferrari for a joy ride. At the end of an amazing day of fun, adventure and intrigue, they return to discover the joy ride clicked off over 100 miles on the odometer. Cameron has a complete emotional meltdown while Ferris attempts to soothe his friend's fears of his father discovering the added miles. When they return home, Ferris has a plan to jack up the rear of the car and run the car in reverse, believing it will roll back the miles on the odometer.

When they realize the odometer is not rolling back, Cameron begins to release his pent-up anger for his father. He stands in front of the car, kicks the car and yells, "Who do you love?" With each angry kick he yells, "Who do you love?" He then takes a step back to see the extensive damage he has done to his father's prized possession and rests his foot on the hood as the car continues to run in reverse. After all of the kicking, the weight of Cameron's foot is enough to push the car off the jack. The spinning tires hit the garage floor, propelling it through the glass wall of the garage, crashing into the ravine below the house.

Cameron, Ferris and Sloane run to the edge of the garage to assess the damage. In shocked silence they stare in disbelief at the rubble that was once one of only 100 prized 1961 Ferrari 250 GT California Spider convertibles.

## Who Do You Love?

Who do you love? By conscious choice or routine neglect, the role in the center of the wheel will influence and shape every relationship in your life and every decision you make. It's your true north—it's the light that guides your race.

In *"Ferris Bueller's Day Off,"* we never see Cameron's father. Introducing his character to the movie would've turned a comedy into a tragedy. Mark Twain once wrote, "What you are doing speaks so loudly in my ears, I can't hear what you are saying." Regardless of whether Cameron's father thought his role as a dad was a priority, his son thought he loved a car more.

Out of curiosity about how men viewed their roles, I conducted a survey asking men to prioritize the roles in their lives. I provided a list of eight roles—brother, career, Christian, community leader, father, friend, husband and son. They were asked to prioritize these roles in order of their priority and importance in their lives.

The results and comments revealed some interesting themes. Six of the eight roles made it to the top of the list as someone's most important role. While there was no definitive pattern of priority in the responses, the results were certainly thought provoking and confirmed that whatever goes in the center of the wheel powerfully influences the course and trajectory of your race.

You couldn't look at the results and comments without a number of thoughts and questions coming to mind. For starters, think about marriage—maybe your marriage. When you get married, you exchange vows. You make a commitment, "For richer or poorer, in sickness and in health, until death do you part." You can't help but wonder what happens over the course of a marriage race to move a man to rank his role as a husband below everything with the exception of community leader.

What about career roles? How much importance do you place on your professional career? You certainly take pride in your career. Few if any would argue that a career isn't an important part of your identity. But what happens to your race if your career rises to the top of the list and becomes the master of every other role in your life?

Looking over the survey results, one by one, you see races full of hurt, confusion and indecision. One respondent wrote, "I think my priorities are out of order." Another said, "I never really thought about how I prioritized my roles. I need to think about this more." Yet another wrote, "It really hurts to look at this."

Who do you love? Ralph Waldo Emerson said, "A person will worship something... Therefore, it behooves us to be careful what we worship, for what we are worshipping we are becoming."[2] They are becoming a reflection of the role in the center of your wheel.

> "A person will worship something... Therefore, it behooves us to be careful what we worship, for what we are worshipping we are becoming."
> —Ralph Waldo Emerson

## A Race Goes Off Course

My son was a freshman football player when Nick was the star senior quarterback at Tesoro High School in Southern California. Nick led the Tesoro Titans football team to a CIF championship. In the spring Nick was a star center fielder on the baseball team and earned all-league honors. Beyond his athletic prowess, Nick was a solid student which added up to a bright future.

Have you ever met people who seem to consistently have it all together? Everything they do is easy and effortless. By every appearance they have their priorities in order and have a command of their future. Then you get a glimpse inside and find out that outward appearances do not reflect the internal story.

Do you think this headline would grab your attention?— "Turning his life around: Former Tesoro High star quarterback went from heroin addict to his mom calling the cops on him."[3] I quickly opened up the article and read about Nick's amazing journey. Nick's athletic ability ultimately landed him a scholarship to the University of Colorado. But, as his race unfolded, it was Nick's private journey with addiction that brought everything crashing down. His most important roles as a son, athlete, teammate, student and coach were thrown to the curb.

Nick's story reflects the fact that some defeat will inevitably enter even the most victorious life. No one runs a perfect race. Sure, you've run some good races, maybe great races that have been satisfying and rewarding. You've also run races that have been littered with mistakes, disappointments and failures—maybe even damaged some of the most important relationships in your life.

Ultimately, you are going to enter the stadium for your last few laps of any number of important races. This is the moment your priorities will be crystal clear because the people gathered in the stands will reflect back how much impact your race had on who and what you loved.

The mere complexity of life exerts never-ending pressure on your roles and how you direct your time, talent and resources. But the greatest of all human freedoms is the freedom to choose. You get to choose which roles are going to command your time and attention. The most important thing you can do to run a great race is to commit your full attention to the development and execution of the roles that give you the best opportunity to positively impact the people you love, the teams you lead and the causes that stir your heart.

## Start Right Where You Are At

In the world of friendly golf, players like to employ the strategy of mulligans. A mulligan is an opportunity to repeat a failed shot and score it as if the poor shot never occurred. On a trip to Ireland one of my friends hit an errant shot on the first tee. He looked at his Irish caddy and asked, "What do you call a mulligan here in Ireland?" Without even a hint of a smile, the caddy pulled a golf ball from his bag, tossed it to my friend and said, "You're hitting three."

When my youngest son was seven and learning how to play golf, he was not familiar with the concept of mulligans. Dissatisfied with a shot, Andrew would request a do-over. His favorite hole for do-over was a par three with a lake between the teeing area and the green. Nothing I could do or say could coax him into moving forward to make the shot easier. Andrew insisted on fully experiencing the thrill of flying the ball over the water, onto the green, from the men's tee.

When we went out to play, he would anxiously anticipate the challenge of his favorite par three. Andrew's focus would sharpen and you could nearly feel his intense determination. Andrew plunked dozens of golf balls in the lake over the years. With each failed shot, he would request a do-over. Not even the greatest motivational genius could have convinced him to move on and try another day. He did not want to hear about the cost of lost golf balls or delaying other players. What Andrew wanted was a do-over.

If life is a game of golf, we have all plunked a few balls in the water. Unfortunately, in life, there are no do-overs. But it is never too late to start a new race. Good or bad, letting go of who you were... in order to become who you have the potential to be begins with understanding and prioritizing your most important roles. Even in the midst of your worst races, there is a familiarity that breeds comfort you won't easily shake.

Nick Nelson lost sight of the important roles in his life and was running a losing race. But his race was not lost. With the help of friends and family, Nick got on the road to recovery and stepped up to a new starting line. Nick has got it right now—roles prioritized and aligned to generate impact. Talking about his new race he said, "This is going to be a great story."[4]

Great stories emerge and take shape when you get your roles in order. Whatever your current circumstance or condition, good or bad, start where you are. You can't roll back time and start over, but you can begin a new race and run towards a brand new ending. Commit yourself to pursuing excellence in the roles that position you to maximize your impact.

## You've Got to Get This Right

> "All we have to decide is what to do with the time that is given us."
> —J.R.R. Tolkien

I often think about Larry telling me, "If you put your family first, you will never be disappointed." Disappointment is the reward waiting for anyone who fails to fully commit to pursuing their most important life roles. Don't lose sight of who you love. Why you love someone or something breaths inspiration into every great race. J.R.R. Tolkien said, "All we have to decide is what to do with the time that is given us." Don't get slowed down or career off your course by leaving the exchange of your precious time and finite resources to chance.

The role you place in the center of the wheel is going to be the lens through which you see and act on every other role in your life. On your mark! When you step up to run the races of life fully committed to excelling in your most important roles, your life will be instantly transformed—you'll know who you are running for. You will see the finish line with renewed vigor, energy and excitement. Choose well, you've got to get this right.

# PART 2

## Get Set!

### "Preparing to Run"

> *"Decide what you want, decide what you are willing to exchange for it. Establish your priorities and go to work."*
> —H. L. Hunt

> *"Hold fast to your dreams! Within your heart keep one still, secret spot where dreams may go, and sheltered so, may thrive and grow. Where doubt and fear are not. Oh keep a place apart, within your heart for little dreams to go! Be not simply good, be good for something."*
> —Henry David Thoreau

> *"Let our fear become courage! Let our timidity become boldness! Let our uncertainty become confidence."*
> —Richard Stern

# CHAPTER 6

## Possibilities: "How Big is Your Box?"

*"Don't put a limit on what can be accomplished...Either you decide to stay in the shallow end of the pool or you go out in the ocean."*
—CHRISTOPHER REEVE

*"The only limits to the possibilities in your life tomorrow are the buts you use today."*
—LES BROWN

Did you ever daydream as a kid? We all did—thinking about amazing achievement and adventure. What about now? Do you ever think about what your life might have looked like if all your childhood dreams had come true? Maybe wished you had a better story to tell at your high school reunion? Perhaps, from time-to-time, dream about what life could look like now if you rekindled your dreams?

Edgar Allen Poe said this about dreams—"Deep into that darkness peering, long I stood there, wondering, fearing, doubting, dreaming dreams no mortal ever dared to dream." Regardless of who we are or where we came from, we dreamed daring dreams about who we were going to be when we grew up.

Remember dreaming about what you wanted to be when you grew up—those golden moments of youth when you proclaimed in front of your classmates who you were going to be when you grew up? We were going to be nurses, lawyers, fire fighters, doctors, inventors and teachers.

In the third grade, I declared my desire to become President of the United States.

Somewhere along the way you abandon bold dreams and ambitions—even in the midst of encouragement. My high school history teacher, Mr. Dan Jones, encouraged me to think big. Mr. Jones recommended that I pursue admission to Harvard University. I knew Harvard was a great university and I knew it was 3,000 miles from home.

Understand, neither of my parents attended college—there was not a college pedigree in my family. After high school most of my classmates would go to work, attend the local community college or enlist in the military. I appreciated Mr. Jones, but I had no idea why he was trying to spur my dreams. He wrote me a tremendous letter of recommendation and helped me pull my Harvard application together.

But somehow dreams of going to Harvard faded into a vision of playing in the NBA. It was a big dream for someone standing just 5' 7". In reality, I had a better chance of becoming President of the United States than playing in the NBA. Goodness, I had a better chance of being President than playing basketball in college, but it did not stop me from dreaming about it.

Believing in my dream, I sought out the coach at Pacific Lutheran University. He encouraged me to come and visit. After the visit and in spite of an average high school career, I thought I had a chance to play basketball at PLU. I remember that Mr. Jones was clearly disappointed when I told him I no longer needed his help to get into Harvard.

I showed up at PLU excited to pursue my basketball dream. After the first week of practice, the coach set up one-on-one meetings with each of the players. When I sat down with coach Anderson, he got right to the point. "Jim, we love your heart. Your energy and enthusiasm are tremendous—these qualities would be an asset to this team. You do some good things. But..." The moment you hear, "But" you don't need an interpreter to tell you this is not going to end well. The simplified message boiled down to, "You're not big, and you're slow." A less than flattering skill combination if your dream is to play basketball.

We all start out with a personal possibility box bursting with glorious expectations—a repository for all your life's hopes and dreams. It reflects your deepest personal aspirations—who you hope to become, circumstances and conditions you desire to change, people you want to influence and causes that stir your hearts.

'Possible' can change quickly in the bright light of reality.

## Under Pressure

"To accomplish great things, we must not only act, but also dream; not only plan, but also believe." Anatole France, the Nobel Prize Laureate, perfectly describes our dilemma. The potential you see and feel peering inside our possibility box fills you with both excitement and apprehension.

Your choice to include a dream in your possibility box, or act upon it is shaped and influenced by many things. Take a moment to think about how your dreams are influenced and you will begin to see how your family, familiar culture, predominant environment, life experiences and time and circumstance have shaped what you think is possible.

## The Shaping Forces of the Experience Cycle

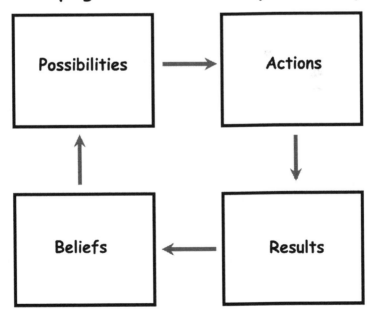

Over time this pattern of experience becomes the blueprint for building your possibility box. The pattern does not require your permission or require your conscious involvement. It consistently repeats itself whether you think about it or not. As you run the varied races of your life, these forces mold and influence your attitudes and beliefs about what you think is possible.

> Your potential to positively impact the people you love, the teams you lead and the causes that stir your heart will be reflected in your ability to maintain a healthy and expanding possibility box.

Unfortunately, over time this cycle of experience is more likely to shrink your possibility box than to expand it. Your potential to positively impact the people you love, the teams you lead and the causes that stir your heart will be reflected in your ability to maintain a healthy and expanding possibility box.

## The Blind Side of Possibilities

The story of Michael Oher, as depicted in *The Blind Side*, is a perfect example of how the forces of family, culture, life experience, time and circumstance and encouragement can influence and shape your possibility box. How could a young man... growing up in a public housing project, without a father, under the oversight of a mother addicted to crack cocaine...pour much more than despair into his possibility box?

In the light of despair, the one thing Michael could see as possible was using his 6' 2", 350-pound frame as a bodyguard for one of the more than two dozen gangs that dominated the landscape of his neighborhood. Attending 11 schools in nine years and missing 51 days of school his freshman year of high school produced a high school GPA of 0.06—an academic track record unlikely to encourage Michael to put a high school diploma in his possibility box. The only race Michael was running was the race for physical survival.

The forces that work to deflate your possibility box ignore your ability and talent. A change in those forces can dramatically affect the races you choose to run and how they unfold. And that is exactly what happened to Michael. With the help of a counselor from a local mentoring program, Michael was accepted into an exclusive college preparatory high school.

Michael did not lack the intelligence to succeed—he lacked the resources. Michael did not lack the athletic ability to succeed—he lacked coaching and direction. Until now, every shaping force in his early life served to kill his dreams and shrink his possibility box. The shift in culture, environment, experience and encouragement that came with a new school and a new family began to pump up Michael's possibility box. Michael shifted from surviving to thriving.

The race to graduation was demanding and filled with many overwhelming moments. Michael said, "You know, I'd never even heard of a lot of this stuff...It was like I was starting school in the 10th grade." Asked about graduating high school, Michael said, "It was unbelievable just to, you know, walk across the stage and shake the principal's hand. I was the first one...out of anybody that I ever knew to, you know, graduate. ...It was...a great experience."

Michael received a scholarship to play football at the University of Mississippi. He began to see the possibility of playing professional football, saying, "I would have dreams all the time about me playing in the NFL. Every day I woke up, I said to myself I'm going to work hard today to get to that next level." Michael Oher developed into an All-American offensive tackle at the University of Mississippi. He was selected in the first round of the 2009 NFL draft by the Baltimore Ravens. Michael completed his rise to professional excellence by helping the Ravens win the Super Bowl in 2013.[1]

Thinking about the forces at work on Michael Oher's possibility box, you could easily conclude there was no hope—Oher is an outlier, a special case where circumstances converged to produce an unexpected but spectacular result. Michael Oher ran an unlikely race. But his race is neither random nor unique.

Josh Levin wrote an article entitled *The Other Blind Sides*. In it he chronicled the stories of a number of other athletes who ran races similar to Oher's including O. C. Brown who earned a football scholarship to Southern Mississippi; Todd Williams of the Tennessee Titans; Patrick Willis of the San Francisco 49'ers; Jeremy Maclin of the Philadelphia Eagles; and Shawn Vanzant who played on Butler University's 2010 NCAA Final Four basketball team.[2]

Michael Lewis, author of *The Blind Side*, said, "Perhaps it wasn't amazing journalistic acumen that led me to the story of *The Blind Side*. Maybe I stumbled onto it because it happens so often."[3] Stories of great impact and accomplishment emerge when you breath life into your possibility boxes.

## Expand Your Possibility Box

> "Whatever you can do, or dream you can, begin it. Boldness has genius, power and magic in it."
> —Johann Wolfgang von Goethe

"Whatever you can do, or dream you can, begin it. Boldness has genius, power and magic in it." Pause for a moment and contemplate these words written by Johann Wolfgang von Goethe again. You can—begin it—fill your possibility box with great dreams and get started. Be bold—there is genius, power, and magic in the dreams that are stirring in your heart.

T. E. Lawrence authored *Seven Pillars of Wisdom* and inspired the critically-acclaimed movie *Lawrence of Arabia*, winner of seven Oscars. Winston Churchill called Lawrence "one of the greatest beings alive in his time."[4] By all accounts, T. E. Lawrence led an extraordinary and accomplished life. Lawrence wrote, "All men dream, but not equally. Those who dream by night in the dusty recesses of their minds, wake in the day to find that it was vanity; but the dreamers of the day are dangerous men, for they may act on their dreams with open eyes, to make them possible."

Your personal impact and influence will be a reflection of the depth and quality of the possibilities you identify and nurture—they set the stage for the great races you'll embrace. What you include in your possibility box can and will change over time, but ultimately you choose the races—push back on any advance that threatens to cripple, crush or silence your dreams.

## Possible Looks Different Over Time

As I was writing this chapter, I went on a trip to visit my father-in-law and attend a wedding of my son's best friend from college. My father-in-law was just a few weeks removed from his 88th birthday. In contrast, the wedding guests were largely a few years removed from college. It was an interesting juxtaposition of the great energy and enthusiasm you feel when breaking from the blocks of the starting line of new races and the sense of reflection you feel when the final finish line comes into view.

## *A possible pinnacle?*

I have found that one of the best ways to find out what people are thinking is to buy them a meal—especially college students. Any meal that does not require heating something up out of a can or boiling water is a sure-fire guarantee to attract a crowd. All it takes is to announce, "I'm buying." Buying a few meals opened the door to spending a lot of time with my son's friends and learning about their hopes, dreams and fears.

At the wedding, it was exciting to hear what they were doing postcollege and what they planned on doing—plenty of possibilities. But one conversation stood out. I couldn't dismiss it. It was one of those conversations that vividly portrays how life's races are influenced and shaped by what you think is possible.

I knew Parker (not his real name) well. He was bright, friendly and engaging. I thought so much of his ability that I hoped to hire him to join my company. I was excited to connect him with my team. As I expected, he made a strong impression during his interviews. My team loved his drive, competitiveness, eagerness to learn and relaxed confidence. Unfortunately, he never joined our team.

When my eye caught Parker's, he immediately walked over to say hello. He was excited to tell me he had just been promoted. Parker described his new role as the pinnacle of his career. "The pinnacle of your career?" I curiously asked. "Yes," he replied, "my dad has a similar position. He has been doing it for 14 years after working towards it for years. I got the job in just a couple years." "Pinnacle?" I asked again! Pressing the "pinnacle" comment for the second time got his attention. I continued, "Are you saying this is as good as it gets? This is the crescendo of your career?"

When you break from the starting line on a new race it should be filled with expansive and exciting possibilities. Early successes are not pinnacles. This is not as good as it gets but provides an unobstructed vantage point where you can see expansive opportunity. If you find yourself in a comfortable and predictable routine you are laboring in the valley—your possibility box is collapsing.

### From the pinnacle to the finish line

Parker was so much different from my 88-year-old father-in-law. Pete wasn't trying to break free from the false security of early success to blaze the trail of new races. Pete was talking openly about the view from the finish line. Is it possible to exhaust life's possibilities at a young age? Is it possible to breath life into new possibilities at an advanced age? I was going to find out.

After returning home, Pete asked me to help him set up a new Garmin navigation unit he had received for his birthday. How ironic to be setting up a navigation unit while talking about his life's journey. "So what did you wish for when you blew out all of those candles on your birthday cake?" I asked. While I was using it as a metaphor to solicit some insight, he mumbled something about not having a birthday cake; then laughed about the personal safety danger of lighting and blowing out 88 candles. I think blowing out 88 candles would scare you and me, too. Then he succinctly and adamantly replied, "See 90!"

He was serious. But I didn't think just getting by for two more years dignified his self-reliant and tough-minded demeanor. So I said, "That's it—just get to 90? Come on, you can do better than that." I pressed the issue with a couple questions, "What do you dream about doing in the next two years? What five things could you do in the next couple years that would create the most joy?"

Pete glossed right over the thought of new possibilities and turned his attention to the finish line. He didn't want to talk about future races and possibilities for impact and joy. Pete wanted to talk about his race and took us back to the beginning in 1927. He described the shaping forces of the Great Depression that became the blueprint for shaping and building his possibility box.

Ultimately, Pete described the one single event that profoundly altered the course of his race. He didn't foresee it. No one did. It was unimaginable. No one plans for it; they just deal with it. In the midst of preparing for retirement, my mother-in-law got sick—very sick. In a matter of months Marlene succumbed to lung cancer. At the time, Pete and Marlene had one grandson. Ultimately, Pete would welcome six more grandchildren into the world.

Pete made one comment about this race-altering event that captivated my attention. "My relationship with all of you (referring to his kids) and my grandchildren would've been different if your mother didn't die." It was evident that this was not the first time he had thought about this, but I think it was the first time he shared it. Then he said, "I can't go back and change things." Pete was right! You can't go back and change things. You can only prepare to move forward—pour new opportunities for impact into your possibility box.

Parker and Pete are eerily similar. Do you see it? While they are at polar opposite positions in the race, they are both stuck. You see that the great possibilities that lie in the future are obscured from view when you hold too tightly to what you have today or can't let go of the past. It is not a question of age. Young or old, the possibilities you see in the future are a matter of perspective—you choose.

T. S. Eliot in his book *The Gidding* wrote, "What we call the beginning is often the end—and to make an end is to make a beginning. The end is where we start from." Beginnings and endings are recurring themes in your race. They signify decision points. You get to decide what goes in your possibility box. You get to decide how you are going to respond to the forces that serve to shape and influence your dreams and aspirations. You get to decide which races you are going to run and how you are going to run them. Your decisions will determine the measure of impact you deliver at the finish line.

> "What we call the beginning is often the end—and to make an end is to make a beginning. The end is where we start from."
> —T. S. Eliot

## So What, Now what?

Epictetus was born into slavery in 55 AD. He worked as a slave until he was 16. His master gave him permission to study philosophy, which allowed him to rise to respectability and eventually secure his personal freedom. In spite of cultural and historical tradition, Epictetus would rise out of slavery to become a great philosopher and thought leader.

Epictetus uttered words that ring as true today as they did nearly 2,000 years ago when he said, "It is not what happens to you that matters, but how you react to it that matters." The modern translation of this great Greek philosopher's sage counsel is, "So what, now what?"—it is all about how you choose to respond to what has happened or is happening.

There is a commercial of a little boy standing at home plate with a bat in one hand and a baseball in the other. He looks at the ball and cries out, "I am the greatest hitter in the world." He tosses the ball up in the air, grabs the bat with both hands, takes a mighty swing at the ball and misses. "Strike one," he declares and again cries out, "I am the greatest hitter in the world." He again tosses the ball in the air, swings and misses. "Strike two," he cries. Readying for a third attempt, he announces, "I am the greatest hitter in the world." The ball rises from his hand, he grabs the bat, swings and misses again. He pauses for a moment—it's a "So what, now what?" moment. "Strike three! I am the greatest pitcher in the world."

Great dreams and possibilities will bring you face to face with the resistance of conventional wisdom. Resistance arising from undue influence based on the experience, knowledge and observations of people who think they are helping you by telling you what you should not or cannot do. Cautious and safe is the harbor of conventional wisdom.

Possibilities and dreams are easily extinguished by well-intentioned people presenting their concern as conventional wisdom. Conventional wisdom too often results in misguided advice—offered by people who are afraid to try themselves or perhaps afraid you will succeed. If you anchor yourself in the safe harbor of conventional wisdom, you'll avoid potential failure and disappointment. But more importantly you'll miss out on running races you need to run to generate meaningful impact.

## Is it Possible?

Possible grows in the fertile soil of "what if" thinking. "What if" thinking is the gateway to new possibilities that lead to greater impact. "What if" thinking pushes aside conventional wisdom and nourishes an attitude of enthusiasm and hope. What if thinking assures you are thinking about possibilities and deliberately planning for impact.

All of the impactful contributions in history would have never been achieved if age (young or old), talent or circumstance would have shaped the thinking. Great and lasting impact is unleashed when you think "what if."

Think you are too young? By the age of 28, Paul McCartney launched his solo career after the Beatles broke up. Nobel prizewinner Milton Friedman completed his doctoral dissertation. Mark Zuckerberg took Facebook public. William Pitt was elected Prime Minister of Britain. Jordan Romero (age 13) climbed Mt. Everest. And Malala Yousafzai (age16) was nominated for a Nobel Peace Prize.

Think you are too old? Julia Childs takes her first cooking class (age 36). Ray Kroc launches McDonald's (age 52). J.R.R. Tolkien publishes the first volume of his fantasy series, *Lord of the Rings* (age 62). Peter Mark Roget publishes the first edition of *Roget's Thesaurus* (age 70). Grandma Moses begins to paint (age 76). John Glenn flies in space (age 77). And Nola Ochs earns a college degree (age 95).

Impossible impact becomes possible the moment you think *what if.* Harriet Thompson would agree. She didn't let conventional wisdom keep her from pursuing greater impact. Harriet is a two-time cancer survivor who took up running marathons at the age of 76. Over the course of her marathon career, she has raised over $100,000 for the Leukemia and Lymphoma Society.[5]

Harriet Thompson turned 76 years old, in 1999. In the face of losing her husband and a number of family members and friends to the ravages of cancer, she decided to do something about it. Thinking about the devastating losses she experienced as a result of cancer, she said, "That makes it personal, something that I really feel is important."[6]

Purpose being the wellspring of possibility inspired Harriet Thompson to enter the Rock 'n' Roll Marathon in San Diego to raise money for the fight against cancer. If Harriet Thompson allowed conventional wisdom to guide her race, she'd be dead—already pushed across the finish line with little fanfare, attention or impact.

An energetic 92-year-old Harriet Thompson lined up to run her 16th Rock 'n' Roll Marathon, in 2015. Again setting aside conventional wisdom, she ran the race with painful wounds on her legs from undergoing radiation treatments earlier in the year for squamous cell carcinoma. Not to be denied the satisfaction of breaking the tape, she completed the race in 7:24:36, just shy of her world record time of 7:07:42. At 92 she became the oldest runner in history to complete a marathon.

> Conventional wisdom doesn't define what is possible—it simply establishes the current boundaries of what you know and have experienced.

Conventional wisdom doesn't define what is possible—it simply establishes the current boundaries of what you know and have experienced. Harriet Thompson knew nothing about running marathons. Harriet's age and health were more than enough to preclude the possibility of running a marathon. You, too, will face circumstances and conditions capable of persuading you to set the pursuit of greater impact aside—don't give in. Embrace new possibilities for impact by utilizing "what if" thinking.

## Crossing the Finish Line

This chapter is about encouraging you to see the future with fresh eyes and a new vision. Set aside conventional wisdom and think about the races you can run that will have the greatest impact on the people you love, the teams you lead and the causes that stir your heart.

Don't look back—you can't run an impactful race looking in the rear view mirror. I can assure you that your potential, capability and capacity for impact is much larger and more expansive than what is contained in your current possibility box.

It is time to clean out the stale and unimportant dreams. Begin to think about remodeling and expanding your platform for impact. Your possibility box doesn't know how your age and how the forces of the experience cycle have affected you. Future possibilities have nothing to do with how well you have run the previous races in your life. Ignore your current resources and circumstances. Don't allow them to be an excuse.

Resources can be acquired and developed. As for circumstances? Positive impact requires you to believe the purpose of your race is greater than your circumstances.

The impact you desire most always flows from your most important roles—those roles that intersect with the people you love and the people who cross your path in your daily life. Stir up your possibilities by thinking deeply about these four questions.

- How would you assess the status of your race performance for each of your most important roles?
- How would people touched by each role and observing your race assess your performance?
- If your role came to an end today, what would be left undone, unsaid or incomplete?
- How would you define "finishing strong" in each role?

The answers to these questions will point you towards new possibilities for not only finishing important and critical races but starting new ones—fresh new possibilities that will spark your energy, inspire your thinking and motivate you to action.

Let me warn you this is not easy. You will look into your newly-expanded and remodeled possibility box, and hard work will be staring back at you. Hard work you can avoid by simply minimizing the potential impact of pursuing new possibilities. Challenges you can side-step by thinking any impact you'd deliver won't be missed—no big deal. Opportunities you can overlook because no one will care or notice if you decided not to run the race because you thought it was going to be too tough.

Don't give in. You were created for a great purpose. Everything you have experienced has prepared you for a great purpose that will guide you towards greater impact and more influence. Purpose and possibility rarely arrives when you want it to. It's not something you dial up, but something you must work to recognize. Tape breakers are possibility alert. They see the same circumstances and conditions everyone else sees with fresh receptivity and turn the seemingly unordinary into something impactful.

*In the face of debt and suffering, why didn't he say no?*

One of the most famous and widely-shared pieces of music in history is *Messiah* composed by George Frideric Handel. Even the most unfamiliar are likely to recognize the famed Hallelujah Chorus. And, after nearly 300 years, performances of the great work continue to attract huge crowds.

Handel was a musical prodigy. He mastered composing for the organ, oboe and violin by the age of 10. While in his teens, he composed church cantatas and chamber music that did not gain much popularity. His father objected to his pursuit of music and insisted George study law. Respecting his father's wishes, he enrolled in law school only to quickly withdraw to pursue his love of music.

Acting on the possibilities flowing from his heart, Handel was a full-time violinist and a composer of operas and oratorios (large-scale concert pieces) by the time he was 18. Handel was recognized by his peers as a genius. Beethoven referred to him as the greatest of composers. In spite of his talent and acclaim, Handel now 57, found himself deeply in debt and struggling to recover from a stroke.

Most people would have thought Handel's best races had already been run when he accepted a token commission to write a production for a charitable performance. Twenty-four days later *Messiah* was complete. One of the greatest musical compositions in history born out of simple possibility. Commenting on his work, Handel said, "I did think I saw all Heaven before me and the great God Himself."[7]

## How Big is Your Possibility Box?

Andy Andrews, in *The Final Summit*, writes, "For if you are breathing, then you are still alive. And if you are still alive, that means you haven't accomplished what you were placed on earth to do. If you haven't accomplished what you were put on earth to accomplish, this signifies that your life's very purpose has yet to be fulfilled. If your very purpose has yet to be fulfilled, that is proof that the most important part of your life remains ahead of you!"[8]

Dreams of high office, professional sports, and grand institutions of higher learning may not come true. But possibilities do not die with them. Great promotions and advancement can happen when we are young, but they are not pinnacles—merely a milestone post. Circumstance and conditions are real, but they do not have to define you. And even when you've entered the stadium for your last few laps and you can see the finish line, if you are breathing, you haven't accomplished all you were placed on this earth to do.

So what, now what? Fill up your possibility box with races that will produce a profound and lasting impact on the people you love, the teams you lead and the causes that stir your heart. Fill your possibility box with dreams that will positively change lives forever. Maybe Edgar Friedenberg, a noted scholar and author, captured it best when he said, "What we must decide is perhaps how we are valuable, rather than how valuable we are."

> "What we must decide is perhaps how we are valuable, rather than how valuable we are."
> —Edgar Friedenberg

Prepare to run. Great impact is the harvest you will enjoy from consistently pouring new dreams into your possibility box.

# CHAPTER 7

## Don't Sit Out: "Developing the Courage to Run"

*"Courage is doing what you're afraid to do. There can be no courage unless you're scared."*
—EDDIE RICKENBACKER, MEDAL OF HONOR RECIPIENT

*"The bravest thing you can do when you are not brave, is to profess courage and act accordingly."*
—CORRA HARRIS, AUTHOR

Stories, movies and pictures of courage stir our emotions and draw our praise and admiration. We easily identify courage with acts of heroism and bravery. We don't see courage as something to draw upon in our everyday lives—not realizing how essential developing personal courage is to creating lasting and meaningful impact.

I think we all want to be brave. Don't you? We crave the courage necessary to push aside our fears. We thirst for opportunities to explore possibilities instead of cowering to our limitations, whether real or perceived. We plead and beg for courage in the face of uncertainty and challenge only to find it only emerges out of practice and experience.

One of my earliest recollections of personal bravery was painful. What most of my friends found fun scared me. But this time I was going to be courageous. This time I was ready. I was finally going to sleep over at my best friend's house. Packing for every contingency, it took me two trips to carry all of my important stuff over to his house. It was going to be awesome. Dennis set up his tent in the backyard and positioned his telescope for exploring the night sky.

Everything was great until the sun went down. It wasn't long before all I could think about was going home. Regardless of the potential ridicule, I decided this was not a time to be brave and courageous. I just needed to go home—now! Just picture me standing in front of Dennis's mom and dad clinging to everything I had brought with me. I'm sure my knees were shaking when I sheepishly explained I had to go home to get something I'd forgotten.

I am sure that they had no doubt I was not coming back. They knew I was scared, but there was nothing they could have done to stop me from making my dash for home. I am glad no one truly expects a six-year-old to be courageous. Thank goodness courage is something we develop.

## Understanding Courage

The celebrated poet and author Maya Angelou wrote, "One isn't necessarily born with courage, but one is born with potential. Without courage, we cannot practice any other virtue with consistency. We can't be kind, true, merciful, generous, or honest." You may not be born with courage but, out of the seed of potential, you crave and desire it—not necessarily heroic courage, but the courage great philosophers and theologians might have called the "special sauce" for great living.

Plato identified courage as one of the four essential virtues, along with wisdom, justice and moderation. C. S. Lewis boldly said, "Courage is not simply one of the virtues, but the form of every virtue at the testing point." Aristotle wrote, "You will never do anything in this world without courage. It is the greatest quality of the mind next to honor."

> "Courage is not simply one of the virtues, but the form of every virtue at the testing point."
> —C. S. Lewis

The English word *courage* comes from the French word *cuer*, or the Latin root *cor*—meaning heart. It is where we get the words of encouragement, "Don't lose heart." M. Scott Peck in *The Road*

*Less Traveled and Beyond* writes, "One of the few things that never ceases to amaze me is how relatively few people understand what courage is. Most people think that courage is the absence of fear. The absence of fear is not courage; the absence of fear is some kind of brain damage. Courage is the capacity to go ahead in spite of the fear, or in spite of the pain."[1]

What great finishes do you envision? Think about the wellspring of satisfaction you feel after a hard-fought victory. Now imagine for a moment the lasting impact you desire to have on the people you love, the teams you lead and the causes that stir your heart. The bridge from your current reality to the future impact you imagine is constructed with courage.

Reality reflects what is in our lives. Our imagination envisions "what if" and waits for the courage to act. Thinking about your current reality, if your life today is pretty much the same five years from now, will you be satisfied? How about ten years from now? When I ask people these questions, I almost immediately witness a change in body language as they project their life into the future. Looking into the future, we can't help but think about what we didn't do.

## Just Imagine the Pain of Regret

Bronnie Ware worked as a palliative care nurse—a calling spent making life as comfortable as possible for patients who are dying. Drawn to their stories, her empathetic ear provided them with an important opportunity to talk about their lives. She began to see a pattern of regrets in their stories that became the foundation for her book *The Top Five Regrets of the Dying.*

> "Twenty years from now you will be more disappointed by the things you did not do than by the ones you did."
> —Mark Twain

The most common regret she heard was, "I wish I'd had the courage to live a life true to myself, not the life others expected of me."[2] It is no wonder that Mark Twain wrote, "Twenty years from now you will be more disappointed by the things you did not do than by the ones you did."

The size and strength of your personal possibility box expands and contracts in proportion to your courage. It takes courage to run unpopular races, to take responsibility for a situation or circumstance not of your choosing, or to take the next step in a race when it would be easier to quit. Without courage, dreams you pour into your possibility box will become line items on your list of regrets.

Dante Gabriel Rossetti, the famous 19th-century poet and artist, was once approached by an elderly man. The old fellow had some sketches and drawings that he wanted Rossetti to look at and tell him if they were any good or if they at least showed potential talent.

Rossetti looked them over carefully. Hoping to provide an encouraging word, he looked at each of the man's drawings. Unfortunately he did not see even a glimmer of artistic talent in the work. But Rossetti was a kind man. He told the elderly man as gently as possible that the pictures were without much value and showed little talent. He was sorry, but he could not lie to the man.

The elderly man was disappointed but seemed to expect Rossetti's judgment. He then apologized for taking up the master's time but would he just look at a few more drawings—these done by a young art student.

Rossetti looked over the second batch of sketches and immediately became enthusiastic over the talent they revealed. "These," he said, "oh, these are good. This young student has great talent. He should be given every help and encouragement in his career as an artist. He has a great future if he will work hard and stick to it."

Rossetti could see that the old fellow was deeply moved. "Who is this fine young artist?" he asked. "Your son?" "No," said the old man sadly. "It is me—40 years ago. If only I had heard your encouragement then! For you see, I got discouraged and gave up—too soon."[3]

Stephen King, the best-selling author, said, "Talent is cheaper than table salt. What separates the talented individual from the successful one is a lot of hard work." Hard work requires courage because when you decide to pursue a great goal, you introduce the possibility of failing. When you step out to run an important race, every flaw in your plan will be exposed. Talent will not save your race—it will be your courage to keep running.

## Unexpected Courage

History provides us with ready opportunities to observe and define courage. The nature of human experience and interaction brings us face to face with loss and failure—the inevitable companions of big dreams and important goals sure to die in the absence of courage.

> "Courage is an inner resolution to go forward despite obstacles; Cowardice is submissive surrender to circumstances. Courage breeds creativity; Cowardice represses fear and is mastered by it. Cowardice asks the question, is it safe? Expediency ask the question, is it politic? Vanity asks the question, is it popular?
> —Martin Luther King Jr.

The course of history and the fate of mankind have been changed by a single act of courage. Over the course of five days in 1865, Edmund G. Ross would read about two events that would change his life but not as he expected. Two events, absent Ross's courage, that would have changed how we remember Abraham Lincoln.

April 9, 1865, marked the surrender of Confederate General Robert E. Lee to Union General Ulysses S. Grant— the Civil War came to an end. Two days later Abraham Lincoln laid out a bold vision of reconciliation and reconstruction, saying, "We simply must begin with, and mold from, disorganized and discordant elements."[4]

Before he could begin this great work, President Abraham Lincoln was assassinated on April 14. Vice President Andrew Johnson would assume the presidency and the challenges associated with a nation torn by war and ideological differences.

Johnson had the courage to stand alone. He demonstrated it as the only member of Congress from a southern state to refuse to secede with his state. Now as President he was determined and resolved to carry out Lincoln's policies and vision of reconstruction.

Johnson's commitment and courage met with opposition from a Congress determined to inflict pain on the defeated Southern states. Congress continued to pass legislation that Johnson vetoed on the grounds of constitutionality, ill-treatment of the South and infringements on the office of the President.

In their attempt to seize control, Congress pressed to secure an iron-clad two-thirds majority in the Senate—a position that would allow them to overturn any presidential veto. When Kansas Senator Jim Lane voted to uphold

Johnson's veto of the Civil Rights Bill, he was condemned by his home state. Humiliated and suffering from ill-health, Lane took his own life.

Edmund Ross, believed to be the secure vote needed for the two-thirds majority vote, was named as Lane's successor. With Ross in place, Congress made plans to impeach Andrew Johnson. Abraham Lincoln said, "Nearly all men can stand adversity, but if you want to test a man's character, give him power."

Ultimately, Ross would cast the swing vote that would determine the outcome of the indictment. The night before the impeachment vote, Ross received a telegram signed by D. R. Anthony and 1,000 others: "Kansas has heard the evidence and demands a conviction of the President." Ross cast the telegram aside by responding, "I do not recognize your right that I vote either for or against conviction. I have taken an oath to do impartial justice according to the Constitution and laws, and trust that I shall have the courage to vote according to the dictates of my judgment and for the highest good of the country."[5]

It was no secret Ross disliked Johnson. Hatred aside, an impeachment vote would surely bring Ross tremendous financial gain and political influence. Everyone counting on Ross believed there was too much for him to gain to vote against impeachment. But Edmund Ross stood alone and voted against impeachment. He surprised everyone with his courage because grave personal consequence was his prize. In the wake of the vote, detractors demonstrated their hatred for Ross and his family. They went out of their way to inflict great personal damage upon him.

It took courage for Ross to run this unlikely and unexpected race. The courageous act of this one man likely preserved the foundational elements of the Republic. Lincoln knew that reconciliation would require the courage of men like Edmund G. Ross when he said, "America will never be destroyed from the outside. If we falter and lose our freedoms, it will be because we destroy ourselves."

If you falter and lose your way, it does not mean certain destruction. Destruction is the path void of courage. The important races you must run in order to fulfill the most impactful roles in your life will be filled with ups and downs. Courage is what will allow you to stand alone and maintain your commitment to finish.

# 3 Steps to Developing Courage

**1. *Fake it until you make it—courage will follow.***
Although faking generally exposes weakness and fraud, faking courage can actually produce it according to Amy Cuddy, a social psychologist and Harvard professor. Cuddy's research shows that you have to "fake it until you become it." Based on Cuddy's research courage to act rises when you make the choice to act confidently until you actually are confident.

When I first viewed Amy's 2012 TED Talk, *Your Body Language Shapes Who You Are*,[6] my mind immediately thought of Charlie Pike. Charlie made himself impossible to forget. He walked into our training room and left an indelible impression. We were all chattering as we found our seats after lunch. Nearly everyone in the room was fresh out of college—just finishing up our first month of sales training.

As the room continued to buzz with conversation, Charlie slowly walked down to the stage. As he reached the center of the stage, he slowly turned around and stood silent. The room got quiet. Fifty sets of eyes fixed on Charlie. Standing center stage, he slowly looked side to side, ensuring he made eye contact with everyone in the room. Feet firmly planted shoulder width, he raised his hands above his head and yelled out, "I feel great." His theatrics rocked us out of our post-lunch drowsiness. Hands still raised above his head, he yelled out again, "I feel great." Charlie continued to exclaim "I feel great" a few dozen times with his hands stretched out over his head.

As Charlie lowered his hands, he explained that selling was a tough profession. He told us that it would beat us down and shake our confidence. He shared stories of how it would rob us of enthusiasm and bring us to the brink of quitting. "On those days where you don't feel your best," he said, "get in front of a mirror and plant your feet. Take a deep breath and raise your hands in the air. Then enthusiastically say I feel great until you are convinced. Then go to work."

He walked up the stairs and took a seat in the back of the room. That was it. In the next few minutes we were dismissed to go to the airport for a month of field training. We laughed and joked for weeks about feeling great. Charlie was right! There are days when it is tough to muster up the courage to run the races you have to run. But, really, who is going to stand in front of a mirror, raise his or her hands and emphatically say "I feel great!"

You should if you want more courage. Charlie was right! Amy Cuddy proved it. Cuddy's research showed that simply posing like Charlie did for two minutes results in a significant physiological change. Cuddy calls it a "power pose," a body position that expands and stretches you whether seated or standing.

Amy Cuddy's research reveals that taking on an expansive physical posture results in a powerful change in our body chemistry. The power pose increased testosterone (the dominance hormone) by 20% while simultaneously reducing cortisol (the major stress hormone) by 25%. Charlie didn't need science to explain what he had experienced. He was onto something big. By simply changing your posture, you can increase your courage—courage that helps you lean into fear and take positive action.

In Cuddy's research, 86% of the people who took on the power pose reported positive feelings about taking chances. In a second group, Cuddy asked the participants to sit and stand passively with their arms and legs crossed. The nonpower posers experienced a 10% drop in testosterone and a 15% increase in cortisol. Accordingly, only 60% demonstrated assertive behavior.

The simple act of changing your body posture will make you more courageous. Cuddy's research didn't test for the impact of shouting "I feel great," but I can tell you from experience it is worth trying.

## 2. Connect align your roles and purpose.

Courage is fueled by great purpose—an inner desire and drive to fulfill the roles that provide you with the greatest opportunity to use your unique talent and skills to maximize your impact.

Personal alignment with and commitment to a great purpose give rise to heroic courage—purpose built upon love so profound you are willing to die for it. Step inside a story for a moment and experience how the alignment of purpose gives rise to courage as part of a team-building program.

> Personal alignment with and commitment to a great purpose give rise to heroic courage—purpose built upon love so profound you are willing to die for it.

Picture yourself sitting in a classroom setting with a group of people who are important to you. You are about to go through a team-building exercise. You are joined in the room by an instructor who tells you the day will be filled with mental, physical and emotional challenges. But by the end of the day you will discover courage that rises from understanding an over-riding purpose.

Your experience begins by watching a collection of Olympic gold-med-al-winning-balance beam performances. You watch these amazing athletes move across the beam with effortless grace. As the last performance fades, a question appears on the screen, "What about you?"

The instructor steps to the front of the room and asks, "What about you? Can you picture yourself on the balance beam?" You and everyone in the room burst out in laughter. You may be a lot of things, but even the best athletes among you do not picture themselves as gymnasts. The instructor motions everyone in the room to follow him outside. As you are walking outside he asks, "How about walking across a four-inch wide, 16-foot long beam positioned seven inches off the ground?"

"Okay," you think—there is little danger in walking across the beam if it is seven inches off the ground. When you get outside, you see a metal beam. Your team is informed it measures 16 feet long but is 16 inches wide—four times as wide as a competitive balance beam. Pull out a ruler if you like but 16 inches is wide enough to stand on with both your feet side by side.

The beam is positioned seven inches off the ground—training height for a beginning balance beam student. The instructor walks over to the beam, steps up and walks the 16-foot length in seconds. You all quickly fol-low and easily navigate your way across the beam—walking, running and skipping.

With one success under your team's belt, the beam is raised four feet off the ground—competition height. Everyone gathers on a platform next to the beam to get a sense of its height. It doesn't seem like much but it raises some concern and anxiety for some of your team members—not you. With a little support and encouragement from the instructor and team members, everyone makes it across the beam.

As your team celebrates and declares victory, the instructor says, "Wait, you're not done." The beam is raised again—20 feet above the ground. It doesn't sound like much until you look up. Even though you are reminded that the beam is still a generous 16 inches wide, it looks like a small fraction of that width when it is suspended 20 feet above the ground. Anyone claiming they are comfortable now would have a tough time passing a polygraph test.

With everyone looking up at the beam, the instructor asks, "Who would take $5 to walk across the beam?" All quiet! You glance away. "$10 dollars...$20 dollars...$50 dollars," he chides. "Hey, you all easily made it across the beam twice—once at seven inches and again at four feet. What is your hesitation? It is the same beam! Does the height of the beam change your ability to walk across the beam?" he probes. "How about $50 for eight feet," one of your teammates quips.

Your ability to walk the beam certainly did not change, but the performance context did. Raising the beam to 20 feet introduced a new element of risk. No one thinks the risk of falling 20 feet is worth a measly $50. But what about for the team? Remember, this is a team-building exercise. Sixteen inches is still 16 inches even at 20 feet above the ground. This is a test of courage. Courage to act in the face of fear and uncertainty.

Your team climbs to the platform at the foot of the beam. Each of you, wearing a tethered harness, easily walk across the beam. The harness provided a measure of comfort and security, but no one had the slightest misstep or hesitancy crossing the beam—even 20 feet above the ground.

The instructor continues to expand the illustration, "This beam now connects two 20-story buildings. Imagine the beam above you being raised another 180 feet—equivalent to a 10-story building. How do you feel? Scared, hesitant, certainly less than courageous. The building you are standing on represents your current strategy. It is going to fail and the building you are standing on is going to crumble to the ground. All of you have to get across this beam to the adjoining building or your team will fail. All in! You succeed together or everyone fails; there are no survivors."

You all begin to joke about finding new jobs. The instructor interrupts your fun. "Failure will not only mean losing your jobs. You'll also lose your family and friends. Your health will suffer. You will lose all of the most important relationships in your life." Well, now that completely changes the game. Your attention and focus is shifted from your immediate personal well-being and safety to the greater purpose of caring for the people you love and lead in your life.

> Courage points you towards something important enough to move you to action in the face of your fear.

See what just happened? When an action is closely aligned with your purpose (most important roles), it ignites the courage within you to act. The courage to start, continue or finish a race is fueled by great purpose. Courage doesn't eliminate your fear. Courage points you towards something important enough to move you to action in the face of your fear.

### 3. A growth mindset builds courage.

Do you ever wake up in the morning and say, "I sure hope I get a chance to struggle and fail today. Wow, that would be fun." It's not fun! Struggles and failures wear you down. You commonly make peace with struggle and potential failure by lowering your performance expectations or abandoning your dreams.

Golf is a game of struggle and failure. Golf proficiency not only requires excellence, it demands it. It becomes a stage for humility and crushes the courage of most who seek to play it professionally. By his own admission, Zach Johnson wasn't even the best player on his high school or college team. His amateur record would not lead anyone to foresee a career in professional golf. He turned pro in 1998 and played on a variety of developmental golf tours for six years before earning a spot to compete on the PGA tour.

His win in the 2007 Masters was considered by most golf historians to be an anomaly. Leading up to the 2015 British Open Championship, no one mentioned Zach Johnson's name as a probable winner. The British bookmakers posted him as a long shot at 66 to 1. At the start of the final round Zach was tied for sixth place, three shots off the lead, but was not mentioned as a player to watch over the course of the final 18 holes.

Zach Johnson eventually emerged from a playoff and won the 144th playing of the Open Championship. By winning on the Old Course at St. Andrews, he became only the fifth player in the history of the game to win The Masters and the British Open at St. Andrews. His name is now etched alongside the legendary golf icons of Sam Snead, Jack Nicklaus, Seve Ballesteros, Nick Faldo and Tiger Woods.[7]

How did Zach Johnson muster up the courage to keep struggling and shake off failure to compile a golf resume worthy of induction into the golf

Hall of Fame? The answer lies in what Zach said when he won The Masters eight years earlier—"I just kept getting better every year." According to Zach's website, he uses an inscription on a homemade ball mark to maintain his improvement perspective: "One shot at a time. Matthew 6:33-34: Seek first the kingdom of God and His righteousness and all these things will be given to you. Do not worry about tomorrow, for tomorrow has enough worry of its own."[8]

> *"Those verses (Matthew 6:33-34) kind of keep me at ease. I don't know if I was communicating with God at the time I was playing, but I felt like I was closer with Him at the time than with anybody else."*
> —ZACH JOHNSON

Courage fuels impact. The courage to persist and get a little better every day is a characteristic that Dr. Carol Dweck has discovered is consistently possessed by high achievers. Dr. Dweck has spent the past two decades conducting research in search of understanding the essential qualities that raise motivation, achievement and success.

Based on Dr. Dweck's research, Zach possesses what she would call a growth mindset versus a fixed mindset. In an interview with the Harvard Business Review, Dr. Dweck defined a fixed mindset as "when people believe their basic qualities, their intelligence, their talents, their abilities, are just fixed traits. They have a certain amount, and that's that." People who possess a growth mindset "believe that even basic talents and abilities can be developed over time through experience, mentorship, and so on. And these are the people who go for it. They're not always worried about how smart they are, how they'll look, what a mistake will mean. They challenge themselves and grow."[9]

Courage emboldens a growth mindset. "The best gift you could ever receive is the encouragement to love and embrace challenges, be intrigued by mistakes, enjoy effort, and keep on learning."[10]

St. Francis de Sales wrote, "Have patience with all things, but chiefly have patience with yourself." You don't need heroic courage that produces an immediately spectacular result. You

> "Have patience with all things, but chiefly have patience with yourself."
> —St. Francis de Sales

need the simple courage to take the next step, to keep running for the finish—the patience that allows you to learn from the struggles and failures you encounter along the way.

## Sitting Out Is Not An Option

Madeleine Albright was the first woman to hold the office of United States Secretary of State. She was born in Czechoslovakia in 1937. Her homeland was ravished with the pain and suffering that accompanies war and political turmoil. A Presidential Medal of Freedom winner, Albright said, "As you go along your road in life you will, if you aim high enough, also meet resistance...but no matter how tough the opposition may seem, have courage still—and persevere."

You will need courage to finish strong. There are reasons why your emotions and mind are stirred by dreams and ambition. They are gifts—the seeds of impact endowed to you to nurture and grow. God places these gifts on your heart. You bring them to life through courage that is lived out in faith. Sydney Smith was an English writer and clergyman who observed, "A great deal of talent is lost to the world for want of a little courage."

Courage is something that is within you. It doesn't require unique talent or special training. It is a commitment to pursuing excellence in the roles you play that position you to have the greatest impact on the people you love, the teams you lead and the causes that stir your heart. Courage doesn't eliminate the uneasy feeling you get when you step out of your comfort zone in the pursuit of meaningful impact. Courage opens the door that allows you to engage in the process of discovering your fuller potential.

Don't sit out. Develop the courage to run!

> When I walk to the edge
> of all the life I have
> and step into
> the darkness of the unknown
> I believe one of two things will happen
> there will be something
> solid for me to stand on
> or I will be taught to fly.[11]
> -S. Marlyn Edges

# CHAPTER 8

# Practice: "Yes, We Are Going to Talk About Practice"

*"Good ideas are not adopted automatically. They must be driven into practice with courageous patience."*
—HYMAN RICKOVER, U. S. NAVY ADMIRAL

*"Practice isn't the thing you do once you're good. It's the thing you do that makes you good."*
—MALCOLM GLADWELL, AUTHOR, OUTLIERS: THE STORY OF SUCCESS

They lost and the city of Philadelphia was reeling in disappointment. The Boston Celtics had just eliminated the championship hopeful Philadelphia 76ers from the 2002 NBA playoffs. Now Allen Iverson had to face a group of Philadelphia sportswriters hungry to find their scapegoat.

Iverson was an all-star. As the reigning league MVP, he was a bona-fide superstar. Allen felt he had left it all on the court in a gut-wrenching loss. As Iverson sat down behind the microphone, the press went on attack. They immediately jumped on a comment from his coach about Allen missing practice.

Pressing Iverson for details, the star player began to rant about practice. "I'm supposed to be the franchise player and we're talking about practice. I mean, listen, we are talking about practice. Not a game! Not a game! Not a game! We're talking about practice...I mean, how silly is that? We're talking about practice...I know it's important. I do. I honestly do. But we're talking about practice...What are we talking about? Practice. We're talking about practice, man!"[1]

Allen Iverson was physically gifted—talented beyond nearly anyone playing in the NBA. He had thrilled the fans with some of the most electrifying and memorable performances in the history of the game. But his Hall of Fame coach, Larry Brown, believed Iverson was capable of leading his team to a championship. In a moment of reflection Larry Brown said, "If A.I. only knew his reach in his time he could have been even bigger than he was."[2]

Yes, I am talking about practice. How would you feel if someone you loved, admired and respected said, "Your potential for impact was greater. You left so many dreams in your possibility box. If you just would've practiced." Can practice make that much difference?

> "For every finish-line tape a runner breaks—complete with the cheers of the crowd and the clicking of hundreds of cameras—there are the hours of hard and often lonely work that rarely gets talked about."
> — Grete Waitz

Grete Waitz was a nine-time NYC marathon champion and former world record holder for the women's marathon. When asked about the key to delivering great performances, Waitz said, "For every finish-line tape a runner breaks—complete with the cheers of the crowd and the clicking of hundreds of cameras—there are the hours of hard and often lonely work that rarely gets talked about."[3]

## Preparation Precedes Performance

Your performance will never exceed your level of preparation. Maintaining focus and commitment to practice and preparation is difficult, but it is the key to achieving high-level performance. I remember asking NHL superstar Teemu Selanne what he thought was the key to sustained performance excellence. He didn't hesitate in responding, "I still prepare like I was a rookie."

Teemu had what most experts would say was the greatest rookie season in NHL history. He won the Calder Trophy as the NHL Rookie of the Year scoring 76 goals and 132 points. Scoring records that are unlikely to ever be broken. What a career—Teemu holds 18 NHL and team franchise records and is the 15th leading scorer in NHL history. He is a six-time Olympian with four medals and the all-time leading scorer in Olympic hockey history. Selanne has hoisted the famed Stanley Cup as a champion and is a lock to be a first-ballot inductee into the Hockey Hall of Fame.

Selanne's talent is undeniable, but it was his commitment to preparation and practice that is special. After his Anaheim Ducks won the Stanley Cup in 2007, Teemu retired from hockey at the age of 37. You could just tell he missed the game. Every time we talked I could hear that he harbored thoughts of returning to the game. Why else would he continue to skate and work out? Midway through the 2008-09 season, the most popular player in Ducks history returned to the delight of the Anaheim fans.

Teemu would frequently say, "It's a young man's game." A true statement as evidenced by only a few players playing at age 40 let alone being key contributors to their team's success. Franklin Steele, an NHL writer and analyst, ranked the top 10 historically best NHL seasons by a player over 40 years old. He rated Selanne's 2010-11 campaign second only to the iconic Gordie Howe. Steele said, "80 points after 40 is one of the most remarkable campaigns by an over-the-hill player in the history of the league."[4]

In his book, *Talent Is Overrated*, Geoff Colvin digs deep into what separates world-class performers from everybody else. Colvin concludes, "The factor that seems to explain the most about great performance is something the researchers call deliberate practice...deliberate practice is hard. It hurts. But it works. More of it equals better performance."[5]

As a friend of Teemu's, I have played golf with him and watched him play tennis—he is simply a remarkably-gifted athlete. But his jovial, relaxed and humble nature could lead you to conclude that his achievements were a reflection of his innate talent. Could deliberate practice have anything to do with it?

I didn't think much about it until Teemu referred me to Dr. Ron Higuera. Dr. Ron worked with most of the Anaheim Ducks players. He is an expert on injury rehabilitation and works regularly with professional athletes. While Dr. Ron helped me solve a persistent elbow problem, I gained some keen insight about the role that practice and preparation play in performance.

It was fun to talk with Dr. Ron about his work with world-class athletes. I was curious to understand how their preparation and practice affected their performance. When I asked Dr. Ron about Teemu, he was quick to acknowledge Teemu's physical giftedness—but then again he worked with a lot of gifted athletes.

> What stands between you and performance excellence in any role is practice—engaging in the process of improvement through quality practice.

"Teemu," he said, "practices and prepares more completely than anyone I have ever worked with. He never stops at the minimum. The young players don't understand what is required to keep their bodies in shape. Their careers will be short because they just aren't committed to excellence. They'd like to be like Teemu, but they don't want to practice and prepare like Teemu."

We're talking about practice. What stands between you and performance excellence in any role is practice—engaging in the process of improvement through quality practice.

## The relationship of practice to performance

Ignacy Paderewski is considered by many to be the finest pianist to ever perform. A musical virtuoso who was discouraged from playing by his teachers. Franklin Delano Roosevelt referred to him as a "modern immortal."[6] Paderewski biographer Charles Phillip wrote, "It is difficult to write of Paderewski without emotion. Statesman, orator, pianist and composer, he is a superlative man, and his genius transcends that of anyone I have ever known...an artist of such a distinctly pronounced individuality as to be an exceedingly rare occurrence—indeed—phenomenal."[7]

Paderewski traveled the world and gave more than 1,500 concerts in the United States—drawing record audiences at a time where solo recitals were rare. Ignacy is said to have been approached by a young woman following a concert. She exclaimed, "I'd give my life to be able to play like you." Ignacy replied, "But my dear lady, I did give my life."

Paderewski understood the relationship of practice to performance. He said, "If I do not practice one day, I notice it. If I do not practice a second day, the orchestra notices it. If I do not practice a third day, the world notices it."

K. Anders Ericsson, a psychologist and researcher from Florida State University, has extensively explored the relationship between practice and performance. He published his research findings in a paper titled *The Role of Deliberate Practice in the Acquisition of Expert Performance.* Ericsson concluded that "...the differences between expert performers and normal adults reflect a life-long period of deliberate effort to improve performance in a specific domain."[8]

## Where Deliberate Effort Can Take You

Even with scientific research telling us talent is not enough how often do we look at great performances and amazing achievements and chalk it up to talent? In high school, I played basketball with Ryne Sandberg—10-time major league baseball all-star, 1984 National League MVP, and 2005 Baseball Hall of Fame inductee.

Ryne's athleticism and talent were obvious. Every move on the field or court was graceful— effortless motion. He was a three-sport star and named to the Parade High School All-American team as a quarterback. He set Spokane high school passing records that were later broken by Super Bowl MVP quarterback Mark Rypien.

When Ryne was drafted in the 20th round of the 1978 amateur baseball draft by the Philadelphia Phillies, many did not consider him to even be the best professional prospect on our high school team—that title would've gone to Chris Henry. Chris was drafted in the 10th round the following year by the Seattle Mariners. Beyond Sandberg and Henry, our high school baseball team included four other players who were selected for first-team, all-city honors.

Vince Grippi, the long-time sportswriter for the Spokesman Review, wrote this about Sandberg in 2005 prior to his Hall of Fame induction—"He was a standout that didn't stand out...good enough to make the Hall? In high school, there were doubts."[9] I knew Ryne well enough to say his talent far exceeded his ego—he never really acknowledged his talent. I acknowledged his talent by nicknaming him "Stud." But he was still just one of the guys. Call him "Stud" and he would typically smile with embarrassing acknowledgement.

Ryne Sandberg did not possess jaw-dropping can't-miss talent, but he did possess exceptional talent. I am fairly confident Ryne never saw himself as a Hall of Fame player. I think he did see himself playing major league baseball. His path to elite performance was paved with hard work, effort and preparation.

> "Talent is God given. Be humble. Fame is man-given. Be grateful. Conceit is self-given. Be careful.
> —John Wooden

It would be easy to point to his talent as the basis for his rise to stardom. But talent is common. What Ryne possessed was an insane commitment to personal excellence and improvement. He consistently sought out and employed the best practice and preparation techniques. Ryne Sandberg is a perfect example of where deliberate practice aimed at personal excellence can take you.

## What is Deliberate Practice

Deliberate practice is foundational to living a life of impact. Charles Kendall Adams, former President of Cornell University, said, "No one ever attains very eminent success by simply doing what is required of him; it is the amount of excellence of what is over and above the required that determines greatness." Practice stretches you and enhances your ability to more effectively live out the important roles in your life.

Your talent and ability are the starting point. Take a hard look at each of your most important roles. What skills and knowledge would you need to acquire or improve in order to raise your performance in these roles? The goal of deliberate practice is twofold—enhance your existing skills and add new skills and knowledge to enable you to improve your performance.

K. Anders Ericsson writes in *The Making of an Expert* that "the journey to truly superior performance is neither for the faint of heart nor for the impatient. The development of genuine expertise requires struggle, sacrifice, and honest, often painful self-assessment. There are no shortcuts... you will need to invest that time wisely, by engaging in 'deliberate' practice—comfort."[10]

Good news...you have talent—undeniable and unique! Even better news is that the research clearly points out that you can achieve excellence—it's up to you. You get to choose what type of race you are going to run and define the impact you want to deliver. But there are no shortcuts when it comes to deliberate

> **Good news... you have talent— undeniable and unique!**

practice. "Doing things we know how to do well is enjoyable, and that's exactly the opposite of what deliberate practice demands. Instead of doing what we're good at, we insistently seek out what we're not good at. Then we identify the painful, difficult activities that will make us better and do those things over and over," as Geoff Colvin writes in *Talent is Overrated.*

For example, you can enjoy working out and building a routine of activities you've mastered that constitute your workout, but this is not deliberate practice. Deliberate practice follows a structured pattern of action and learning that pushes you to go beyond routine and comfortable. It is different from practice that focuses on the repetition of what is familiar—it is not inherently fun.

The pioneering aviator and polar explorer, Admiral Richard E. Byrd, said, "Few men during their lifetime come anywhere near exhausting the resources dwelling within them. There are deep wells of strength that are never used." Use these deep wells of strength to engage in deliberate practice targeted at increasing your performance capacity. No one becomes an expert performer in any role without engaging in deliberate practice—talent and good intentions are not enough.

Engaging in deliberate practice increases your capacity for impact. After a broad and extensive review of performance research, K. Anders Ericsson observes, "The maximal level of performance for individuals in a given domain is not attained automatically as function of extended experience, but the level of performance can be increased even by highly experienced individuals as a result of deliberate efforts to improve."[11]

Think for a moment about Allen Iverson's rant about practice. His team has just been knocked out of the NBA playoffs—the goal to win a championship has ended. "We're talking about practice. I mean, listen, we are talking about practice. Not a game!...," Iverson exclaims nearly two dozen times in response to a question about practice. Could deliberate practice have lifted Allen Iverson and his 76er teammates to an NBA title?

We will never know. But we do know that six-time NBA champion Michael Jordan said, "I've always believed that if you put in the work, the results will come...step by step. I can't think of any other way of accomplishing anything."

Have you ever been captivated by a great speech? Marveled at someone's ability to command an audience and deliver a powerful message—maybe even concluded they possessed a gift you didn't? I remember really enjoying a presentation by one of my managers. As everyone applauded her marvelous presentation one of her peers leaned over and said, "Jeanette is such a great presenter. I wish I had a talent for speaking."

It wasn't that long ago it was Jeanette who said, "I wish I had a talent for speaking." "You do," I said, "you just have to develop it." I suggested Jeanette join Toastmasters. Jeanette recognized improving her speaking skills would increase her professional impact. Toastmasters gave her the opportunity to practice—difficult, uncomfortable, and challenging practice.

Everyone can grow in their most important roles and escalate their impact by following four critical steps.[12]

## Four Steps of Deliberate Practice

### 1. Commitment to improve.

The first step to extending or acquiring new skills and knowledge may be the most difficult—commit. Merely uttering "commitment" is enough to scare most of us. Especially when it will most assuredly push you out of your comfort zone and beyond your current level of competency.

When my first son was born, I was excited. I pictured my youth and what I wanted most from my dad. I saw myself coaching baseball, attending sporting events, having a buddy to play golf with, and proudly sitting in the stands during his games.

In Matthew's younger years he did not have a lot of interest in sports. One day he acknowledged my exasperation in his lack of interest in my agenda and said, "Dad, I guess I am just not a sports guy." "Not a sports guy," I thought, "Tell me this isn't so!" We must have brought the wrong child home from the hospital—"Not a sports guy?"

I had already painted the vision of my role as a father. Four simple words, "Not a sports guy," had just shattered everything I had dreamed being a father would be. I'll change him, I thought. Wait a minute—hadn't I been trying to influence him from the start? Indeed I had. That's when it hit me. "Pay attention," Dad, "he's not buying any of it."

My image of fatherhood took a significant blow. But it didn't change my role. If I wanted to excel in my role as a dad, I had to change. It didn't come easy. I thought more than once, "Of all the qualities he could possibly inherit from me, he was blessed with stubborn determination—really, argh."

So in order to grow in my role as a dad, I had to make a commitment to change. I had to practice and study the things Matthew was interested in. This took me completely out of my comfort zone. I wasn't interested in what he loved, but I was motivated by my desire to be a great dad. To increase my impact as a dad required a commitment to improve—to get out of my comfort zone.

The path of deliberate practice begins with your commitment and motivation to improve in the roles that matter most.

## 2. Build a plan.

What comes to mind when you think of being deliberate? Deliberate means not acting impulsively—fully consider what needs to be done. It is consciously and intentionally building a plan.

Start with your current level of skill and knowledge and understanding what you are doing and why you are doing it. The objective is to build a plan that defines the impact you want to have over the course of the race and how you want to finish.

My plan turned into what I called my "Daddy Development Plan." I created it three years after Matthew was born. It began to take shape by wrestling with this question, "How is Matthew unique?" Matthew didn't need to understand me. It was my role to understand him. You can improve in any significant relational role by focusing on understanding the people you are trying to impact.

I had spent so much time trying to get him to see my world that I hadn't spent any time trying to see the world through his eyes. My vision of golfing and baseball games was replaced with trips to the zoo and wild animal parks. My goals and aspirations for our relationship became our goals. We built our plan around activities that lent themselves to Matthew's interests and curiosity. It gave me the best chance to grow in my role as a dad—to build a relationship with my son. By changing my perspective, I now had a foundation for positively impacting Matthew's life.

> If you want to increase your impact on people, you have to build a plan that allows you to connect with them versus expecting them to connect with you.

If you want to increase your impact on people, you have to build a plan that allows you to connect with them versus expecting them to connect with you.

### 3. Create a feedback loop.

The third step is creating a feedback loop that allows you to know if you are executing your plan. In the absence of timely and informative feedback improvement stalls and performance suffers. Research consistently identifies that feedback from a knowledgeable coach speeds learning and improvement. More on that in the next chapter.

Feedback has been called the breakfast of champions. Feedback fuels great performance because it serves as a scoreboard. How do you measure progress and improvement? You need a scoreboard. In the absence of feedback, your natural inclination is to assume that you are doing a great job, right?

Seeking and receiving feedback holds you accountable to your vision and definition of success. The question I had at the top of my "Daddy Development Plan" was "how to make it work?" My answer was, "Be accountable to Kristi (my wife), Matthew and Andrew, another father, and a fathering group.

Do you know what happens when you tell a kid you are going to go to the San Diego Zoo? Right, they remind you with relentless energy and enthusiasm. And you know what? The more I went to the zoo the better I got at managing the whole experience. Candidly, I didn't like the zoo—still don't. But I loved what it was doing for my relationship with my family.

Deliberate practice in the pursuit of developing a specific talent or expertise requires timely and quality feedback. To improve in your role as a father, mother, husband, wife, runner, musician, golfer, tennis player, leader, coach or any other role—create an effective feedback loop.

### 4. Build practice and engagement into your schedule.

Simple or casual attention to improvement in the roles that have the greatest potential for impact will not get the job done. The old adage was practice makes perfect. What the research clearly tells us is that practice makes permanent. Imperfect or incomplete practice will not lead to improvement that raises impact.

Up until my boys were teenagers, Friday night was guys' night out. When they were young, this was incredibly valuable for two reasons. First, it gave me time alone with them. Second, it gave time for my wife to catch her breath and have some time for herself. Practice and engagement built into your schedule generates significant benefits.

Malcolm Gladwell, in his book Outliers, made the research about deliberate practice famous when he cited the 10,000-hour rule. The rule reflected that great masters, experts and pioneers commonly engaged in 10,000 hours of practice on their journey to role mastery.

Every role you play possesses the seed of incredible impact, but it won't take root unless you schedule time for practice and improvement. Will Smith, the award-winning actor, producer and songwriter when asked about his success, said, "I've always considered myself to be just average talent, and what I have is a ridiculous insane obsession for practice and preparation."

> "I've always considered myself to be just average talent, and what I have is a ridiculous insane obsession for practice and preparation."
> —Will Smith

What would happen if you embraced a ridiculously insane obsession for practice and preparation? What would happen is your personal efficiency and effectiveness would rise—your impact would increase.

## The Rest of the Story

The pursuit of deliberate practice is not fun, but it is critical for personal impact. It is not simple in nature nor merely repetitive. It requires commitment, planning, feedback and scheduling.

Anne Frank wrote, "Everyone has inside of him a piece of good news. The good news is that you don't know how great you can be! How much you can love! What you can accomplish! And what your potential is!" Ignacy Paderewski lived as if he knew no limits. As I close out this chapter, let me share the rest of Ignacy Paderewski's incredible story. It was Paderewski who said he gave his life in order to achieve his musical mastery and brilliance. But that is not the only contribution Ignacy Paderewski made during his life.

With great gifts comes great responsibility. Your gifts are blessing to be used for positive impact. How are you going to use your unique talent to run a great race and maximize your impact? Don't dismiss your preparation and practice lightly—they are preparing you for great new opportunities and responsibilities. Difficulty, pain and discomfort are the seeds of a great purpose. If you embrace them, they can lead to delivering lasting impact in the roles that matter most to you.

Paderewski was committed to delivering impact. His practice in the pursuit of excellence prepared him to run an energetic, passionate and visionary race. Clearly, Ignacy Paderewski was a musical icon. "He was known for having perfected the touch that could literally make the piano sing. His pedaling was also perfect and his musical renderings, no matter how different, were the fruit of profound and serious study."[13] Through the practice and development of his musical skills, he earned more money than any musician in history. Paderewski quietly amassed a fortune.

As magnificent as his music was, it only served as a foundation for what would define his impact and legacy. Paderewski's native Poland was devastated by war. Out of his love for people, Paderewski depleted nearly all of his resources in pursuit of Polish independence. "A humanitarian who was so generous that every act of kindness to him was always returned manifold."[14]

Paderewski was the consummate patriot and an intellectual giant. His musical reputation opened doors to world leaders. The Versailles Peace Treaty was signed in 1919 ending World War I. The treaty restored Polish sovereignty after more than 120 years. Paderewski became the first Prime Minister of the new independent Poland. The Polish people had so much faith and trust in him that they granted him complete authority in all national political matters.

The ever-passionate Paderewski addressed the League of Nations in New York for more than an hour without notes and then repeated his speech in English. Having exhausted all of his resources, Paderewski resigned all of his political appointments in 1922. He resumed his musical career—attracting huge crowds. In 1932, he performed in front of 15,000 people at Madison Square Garden raising $37,000 (equivalent to more than $600,000 in 2015) for support of unemployed American musicians.[15]

Ignacy was 79 years old when World War II broke out. When Poland was invaded, he was again moved to act. In spite of his poor health, he returned to Europe to again support his native Poland. From his home in Switzerland, he established a refuge for emigres and led anti-Nazi campaigns.

Ignacy's dangerous work eventually threatened his safety and well-being. Paderewski was evacuated from his home in November of 1941 and returned to the United States. His failing health claimed his life seven months later. The beloved and admired Paderewski's funeral was held at St. Patrick's Cathedral in New York City. It wasn't a stadium, but they needed one. Over 40,000 people showed up to honor and acknowledge Ignacy Paderewski breaking the tape of an incredibly impactful race.

By presidential decree, an action taken only one other time in U. S. history, he was buried at Arlington National Cemetery. When Poland gained its independence in 1992, Ignacy Paderewski's body was transported back to his homeland for final burial.

Ignacy Jan Paderewski ran a great race. He finished strong. Ignacy truly impacted the people he loved, the people he led, and the causes that stirred his heart. Without question, Ignacy was blessed with exceptional talent. Rare talent that was refined and developed through deliberate practice.

You don't know how great you can be—how much impact you can create. No one does. Inside you is a piece of good news. Deliberately practice what is necessary to grow in your most important roles and discover your capacity for life-changing impact.

# CHAPTER 9

# "Who's Your Coach?: "The Secret to Great Preparation"

*"I never cease to be amazed at the power of the coaching process to draw out the skills or talent that was previously hidden within an individual, and which invariably finds a way to solve a problem previously thought unsolvable."*[1]
—JOHN RUSSELL, MANAGING DIRECTOR, HARLEY-DAVIDSON EUROPE LTD.

*"I absolutely believe that people, unless coached, never reach their maximum capabilities."*[2]
—BOB NARDELLI, FORMER CEO, HOME DEPOT

I was sitting in the front row. The perfect location to avoid distractions. You set a good example when you sit up front. It's the place to get focused and be focused upon. An opportunity in the right light to be noticed. Maybe recognized or even acknowledged by important people. I was present, focused and ready to go—so I thought.

As the session started, my mind started to wander. Fighting drowsiness, I tried not to nod off. You know that feeling when your eyes close briefly and your head begins to fall backwards setting off an internal alarm that suddenly snaps you back to attention. The key, at this point, is to act like nothing happened. Too late, you look around to observe other people being entertained by your act.

Here we go again. My eyes blinked up and down and then fell shut. My head began to fall back. Before the alarm went off and I could snap back from my cat nap, I was startled to attention. "Jim, what do great coaches do?" came the voice from the stage. Front row! Great, I've been noticed—sleeping.

"Are you talking to me?" I thought. A quick glance around to see all eyes staring at me validated that, yes, he was indeed talking to me. Thankfully, I kept my next thought to myself, "Ah, great coaches wake people up who fall asleep during their presentation."

Great coaches do grab your attention. They take players to places they could not go on their own. Coaches are the secret to preparing and developing your capacity and capability to run a great race filled with personal and professional impact.

## Observing A Coach in Action

Have you ever walked on a railroad track? My grandpa made his living working for the SOO Line Railroad. A Norwegian immigrant, he settled in North Dakota where he laid and repaired train tracks. The North Dakota winters made him tough and resilient. Twelve kids molded him into a great coach.

During a summer visit, I remember my cousins and I walking along the train tracks with my grandpa. We would stand on one rail and see who could walk the farthest without falling off. We employed every imaginable strategy—slow, fast, big steps and small steps. Regardless, we could only manage to walk a few feet before our small feet slipped off the two-and-one-half-inch wide rail.

My grandpa was entertained by our persistent and competitive nature. Eventually he took one of my cousin's hands. He stood on one rail, had her stand on the other rail, reached out and took her hand. Then they took off walking. Not just a few feet. Simply by the magic of holding hands, it appeared they could have walked forever.

My grandpa coached by example and demonstration. He helped us to do something we could not do on our own. He demonstrated a powerful truth that is captured in the African proverb, "If you want to go fast, go alone. If you want to go far, go together." If you want to run a race that maximizes your potential impact, you can't do it alone.

## More Than a Snowman

When I was young I tried to do everything on my own. Who doesn't? It's what you do—right? You instinctively strive to become self-sufficient and self-reliant. You declare your desire to learn and grow the first time you say, "Let me do it" or "I know how to do this!" Born with this innate drive for empowerment and competence, it is natural to push coaching and assistance aside.

Who hasn't said, "I don't need a coach. I can do this on my own." There is a certain degree of pride and satisfaction that comes from knowing you did something on your own. When progress is slow and achievement fleeting, it becomes stubborn pride—a sense of determination spurring on great effort and commitment, but it cannot overcome the lack of knowledge and direction.

For me, I wanted people to think I was better than I really was. So not asking for help allowed me to maintain my false sense of control. There was nothing that stood between me and my inflated assessment of my ability. It began to change after a particularly disappointing informal basketball workout during my freshman year at Pacific Lutheran University. I wanted desperately to make the team, but with each passing workout it was becoming painfully obvious the sun was setting on my dream. One of the seniors approached me as we were leaving the gym and asked if I was going to attend the Fellowship of Christian Athletes meeting the following morning.

"Why?" I asked. "Simple. Frosty is going to be there," he said. "Frosty? Who is Frosty?" I asked. He replied, "Just make sure you're there." Under my breath I muttered, "Great, not only am I not going to make the team, now they want to introduce me to Frosty the Snowman."

When my alarm shook me from a deep comfortable sleep I reached over with the thought of hitting the snooze button. Reluctantly I climbed out of bed and looked outside to see a steady pelting rain blowing up against the window of my dorm room. Perfect weather for a snowman! Cold, wet and dark—did I need any more excuses for going back to bed? I showered and got dressed. I looked outside one more time, hoping the rain had stopped. With the words "Just make sure you're there" chiming in my head, I reluctantly stepped out the door.

The cold rain was coming down hard as I jogged across campus to the meeting. I walked in and to my surprise no one else had been deterred by the weather—the room was overflowing. I immediately thought, "Frosty must be the real thing to command this much respect and attention at o'dark hundred."

Great coaches take you to places you could not go on your own. A great coach helps you maximize the quality and depth of your strengths. They provide the watchful eye necessary to guide your development. Great coaches support you through the process of deliberate practice. You need a coach to broaden and enrich your skills and make your weaknesses irrelevant.

On that wet, cold and dark morning in 1977 my eyes were opened to a secret of great preparation—the influence and impact of great coaching. Frosty never talked about football, but he was the football coach. Frosty didn't talk about his success, but his career was filled with achievement and awards. Pondering the over 400 hours of classroom time spent at PLU, I don't remember any of my professors' names or much of anything that I experienced. But I will never forget spending that early October morning in Frosty's classroom.

It was clear no one dragged Frosty to this meeting. It may have been miserable outside, but inside it was coaching time for Frosty. His smile made me feel welcome. Frosty's words filled me with hope. My images of Frosty are indelible. I was looking at strength, belief, passion, possibility and discipline. Frosty was on a journey to personal excellence and extended an offer for everyone to join him. A race of faith built upon the gift of grace and the knowledge that our Creator placed within you the seeds of infinite and amazing potential. For Frosty, it all started with relationship. He lived for the opportunity to be your coach—to help you reach your God-given purpose and potential.

Frosty's team started Fall football camp with what he called "Breakaway"—a three-day retreat on the Oregon coast to get away from campus and football. Over the course of three days, they never touched a football, reviewed a play book or talked game strategy. They spent the entire time forging relationships and building community. Frosty was mentally preparing them for the journey. Players returned, focused on closing what Frosty referred to as the "GAP - the difference between your performance (I am zone), and your potential (I can be zone)."[3]

Frosty said, "It's our ability to choose our actions and reactions in our daily lives that frees us up to experience the natural highs that God intended us to have...the real measurement of who you are is not what you can do in comparison to others, but what you can do in comparison to your own best self."[4]

> ...the real measurement of who you are is not what you can do in comparison to others, but what you can do in comparison to your own best self.
> —Frosty Westering

Frosty pursued excellence in his career as a football coach. Frosty lived out excellence by embracing his calling as a coach to positively impact people—to change your life forever. Frosty was intent upon equipping you to run your races with endurance and courage. He understood that coaching effectiveness required getting you to focus on the process of discovery and improvement. Coach Westering understood that, through deliberate practice, preparation and support, the results would take care of themselves.

Frosty's teams produced results. Frosty is only one of eleven college football coaches to win 300 games, and he ranks in the top ten, all-time, for winning percentage in college football history. His teams produced 32 consecutive winning seasons and he was named National Coach of the Year three times. A coaching resume that landed Coach Frosty Westering in the College Football Hall of Fame.[5]

Frosty infused you with the confidence to pursue your potential. Marcus Buckingham, in *The One Thing You Need to Know*, points out, "People with a slightly unrealistic confidence in their abilities outperform those whose self-assessments are more realistic."[6] Realistic self-assessment is what Frosty calls the "I am zone." It represents your current performance ceiling but not your performance potential. When your confidence is high, even slightly unrealistic, you can raise performance and move to the "I can be zone."

Dr. Jason Selk is an exceptional performance coach. Jason describes his coaching focus as "the relentless pursuit of greatness...developing mental toughness in sport, business, and life." Selk helped coach the 2006 St. Louis Cardinals to their first World Series victory in over 20 years. In the *10 Minute Toughness: The Mental Training Program for Winning Before the Game Begins*, Dr. Selk writes, "The two most effective ways to develop self-confidence are to perform well and to physically and mentally prepare to perform well."[7]

Engaging the support of a coach is essential to your race preparation. Coaches help you improve efficiency, effectiveness and performance.

## The Key Ingredient to Performance Improvement

You have talent! Undeniable talents you may be aware of and some you have yet to discover. You have packed your possibility box with goals and dreams that God has placed on your heart. Be reminded again, dreams do not know how old you are—young or old your age is irrelevant. Every role you play is full of incredible opportunities for impact. The roles of your life do not come with expiration dates. Every breath you take confirms, in the present moment that you have a responsibility to improve the cadence and performance of your race.

In 1985, Dr. Benjamin Bloom published landmark research in a book entitled *Developing Talent in Young People*. Bloom studied 120 highly-accomplished young people, including musicians, athletes, mathematicians, artists and research neurologists. From their work, Bloom and his team drew some powerful conclusions about peak performance from their work.

First, talent was not the essential or primary attribute of the peak performers they studied. Beyond their talent, the participants in the study possessed qualities commonly associated with high achievement, including persistence, competitiveness, passion and commitment. But the most interesting conclusion from their research was discovering the key ingredient of the elite performance formula—coaching.

These world-class performers' pursuit of excellence was not a solo journey or a do-it-yourself project. Peter Drucker, the iconic business and achievement guru, wrote, "The key choices you make—apart from the natural talent you already have—will set you apart from others who have talent alone."[8] Choosing to engage the support of coaches set them apart from those with talent alone. Working with a coach was the key to accelerating their level of interest and commitment to learning.

> "The key choices you make—apart from the natural talent you already have—will set you apart from others who have talent alone."
> —Peter Drucker

### Two essential sources for coaching

Bloom further discovered that coaching came from two different sources. It should not come as a surprise that the first source of coaching was parents. Parents who heard "I can do it" willingly encouraged exploration and growth. Most of the parents did not possess subject-matter expertise. What they possessed was the invaluable voice of encouragement. One of the critical conclusions of Bloom's research is "greatness is uncovered and developed through the cultivation of relationships with coaches." Performance thrives with encouragement when the source of the encouragement is someone who is loved and trusted.

Encouragement fosters enthusiasm and commitment but, on its own, did not lead to excellence. The second critical source of coaching was from subject-matter experts. When student learning was guided by an expert, performance rose. The presence and oversight of an expert to provide timely feedback and instruction were essential to producing performance excellence.

The higher you set your goal for mastery or excellence in a particular role the greater benefit derived from expert coaching. Plato learned from Socrates, and Aristotle was Plato's best student. Wolfgang Mozart is one of the most prolific and influential classical music composers in history. He was encouraged to develop his prolific talent under the watchful eye of his father, Leopold Mozart, who was an extraordinary teacher and a world-class composer, conductor and violinist.

Mozart's talent was undeniable. But his mastery was the reflection of great coaching. Mozart looked to and learned from Bach, Handel and Haydn. Mozart studied the work of the master composers. He sometimes took familiar phrases from the works of other composers and worked them into his own. When Mozart was 28 and Haydn 52, they co-headlined a charity concert in Vienna.[9] Preparation guided by a coach is critical to improving performance.

## *Mastery evolves from great coaching*

How frequently do you engage a coach or expert support? My curiosity about using coaches led to me to conduct an informal survey. I asked, "In order of personal preference, where are you most likely to go to look for new information or resources when looking for an answer or trying to solve a problem?"

Over 50% of the nearly 200 respondents selected "Google it and look for things that fit." In a study by First Monday, a peer-reviewed journal on the Internet, they concluded, 66% of college students used the internet to "find information about making decisions directly related to their individual lives." A focus group participant in the study commented, "Google is always my first step, even though I know it may not be the best first step, but it is my most accessible one."[10]

> "Our chief want in life is to find someone who will make us do what we can."
> —Ralph Waldo Emerson

Ralph Waldo Emerson once said, "Our chief want in life is to find someone who will make us do what we can." Coaching is the secret to great preparation and performance. Our chief want is to find a coach capable of pushing us towards the "I can be zone." Think about a time where you enjoyed a period of important personal or professional growth. Who came alongside you as a coach and helped you realize you could do more? I can't imagine Emerson being so enamored with the Internet that he would say, "Our chief want in life can be found by 'Googling it'."

You, the people you love and the teams you lead will face a future that will require skills and knowledge you do not possess today. Eric Hoffer, author and Presidential Medal of Freedom recipient, wrote, "In times of change, learners inherit the earth, while the learned find themselves beautifully equipped, to deal with a world that no longer exists." In every role of your life, engaging a coach will help you run faster and more effectively. Coaches equip you to run your best race—equipping you with tools, knowledge, training and feedback essential for breaking through performance and contribution barriers.

## The Mindset of a Player

To effectively use a coach requires a teachable spirit—a willingness to get comfortable being uncomfortable. Allowing yourself to set aside what you know and start over. Valuing curiosity over experience. Being willing to ask the question you think even a beginner wouldn't ask.

I recently visited the beginner lane on a visit to the Apple store. I had searched the Internet long enough for a solution to the perpetual wheel of death that spun out of control on my wife's Mac computer. Maybe you have seen it—a rainbow of spinning colors that if it had a voice would shout, "So sorry you are too dumb to figure this out. Please return to the beginner lane."

Who likes to admit to needing help? I don't—do you? And even when you conclude you need help who wants to line up in the beginner lane? We entered the store and my wife, readily admitting she was comfortable being uncomfortable, asked, "Who should we ask for help?" Not yet ready admit the obvious I said, "Follow me." We walked over to the Mac area. I immediately did what everyone does in the Apple store—I acted like I knew what I was doing.

After a couple minutes looking at the new computer options, I said to my wife, "I have no idea what to do." Warming to the idea of getting comfortable with my discomfort, I spotted a rare site—an unoccupied Apple employee easily identifiable by the Apple logo on his blue t-shirt. I introduced myself to Nick, who I later found out was a trainer (aka expert) and not a salesperson, who stepped in as our coach.

It dawned on me very quickly that there was nothing I could say that was going to impress Nick. Even though I had been a Mac enthusiast dating back to the introduction of Apple's first computer —I was a beginner. The more comfortable I became asking what were obviously routine questions for Nick, the more we learned.

Thank you, Nick, I could have spent hours in the Apple store shunning assistance. I might have continued to try to solve the problem on my own if my wife hadn't been with me. She gave me a bit of time to mess around before she again gently suggested asking for help. Ah, the power of coaching. The fastest path to improvement opens up when a teachable spirit is joined with a knowledgeable coach—and a nudge from your wife.

> The fastest path to improvement opens up when a teachable spirit is joined with a knowledgeable coach

## Why Are Coaches the Secret to Great Preparation?

Coaches are vital to your ability to increase your impact on the people you love, the teams you lead and the causes that stir your heart.

Reese Witherspoon won the 2006 Academy Award for Best Actress for her role as June Carter in the movie *Walk the Line.* The film follows the early life of American music legend Johnny Cash, his rise to fame, tumultuous struggle with amphetamines, barbiturates and alcohol and how June's devotion and support saved his life.

Reese entered the role confident in her ability to sing and reflect the vocal quality of June Carter. After hearing her first recordings played back she called her attorney and asked him to get her out of the film. But the producer of the film wouldn't let her quit. Reese said, "After many arguments and discussions they finally made me go back and start working with a vocal coach. It took me five months to get to the point where I could actually hear the playback and it didn't sound like nails on a chalkboard...But with the right kind of coaching and determination you can accomplish anything and the biggest accomplishment that I feel I got from the film was overcoming that fear."[11]

Reese was selected for the role of June Carter based on her potential. The path to becoming an Academy Award-winning actress was unlocked by a coach.

# Five Ways Coaches Help You Unlock Your Impact Potential

## 1. *Assess*

Sparky Anderson knew something about coaching, winning five league championships and three World Series titles managing the Cincinnati Reds and Detroit Tigers. Sparky said, "Good seasons start with good beginnings." Good beginnings require a sound assessment of the players' current ability. You have to understand their potential to perform and reach targeted goals.

A coaching assessment explores a variety of things, including strengths and weaknesses. An in-depth assessment will also explore ambition, perceived obstacles, current circumstances, potential blindspots, and performance history. Depending on what you are trying to achieve, a coach may utilize an external assessment test designed to measure a learning or behavioral style, health or nutritional well-being, academic readiness or physical fitness, to name a few.

A primary reason we do not enlist the support of a coach is because assessment leads to feedback. Can we agree that, even when you ask for feedback, you fear it? Don't you? What if the feedback isn't flattering? What if the assessment paints a picture different from how you see yourself? The answer to this question is easy—obviously the assessment is wrong. Who hasn't received a coaching assessment and rejected it?

I heard a fitness speaker telling the story of a man who was not feeling well. After weeks of feeling poorly and lacking energy, he went to his doctor for a complete physical exam. The next week when he returned to review the results, he immediately took control of the conversation. "Doctor, save all the medical explanations. Just give it to me in plain English. What seems to be the problem?" Accepting the invitation for candid feedback, the doctor replied, "You're overweight, out of shape, and you're diet stinks." Not phased, the man replied, "Now can you give it to me in technical terms so I can explain it to my friends?"

A coach helps you accurately assess your starting position.

## 2. *Plan*

Planning is the art of piecing together the critical actions and behaviors necessary to achieve a specific performance goal. Seeing the future is a visionary activity. The challenge of painting a vision of the future is the immediacy of the moment. Our insatiable appetite for instant gratification fixes our attention on our current performance.

A coach builds the future by design—creating a compelling vision. Dewitt Jones is an award-winning photographer and amazing speaker. I heard him speak on the topic of vision. Jones demonstrated the power of vision using dazzling photography. If a picture is worth a thousand words, his pictures were worth much more. He offered a definition of vision I have never forgotten. Dewitt said, "Vision is the ability to see what everyone else sees and to see something different."

> A coach does something for you that you can't do for yourself—build and support a plan that bridges your current reality with your envisioned future.

While you focus on where you are, a coach has the vision to see where you can go. Remember the picture of the sigmoid curve depicting your race. A coach looks at you and sees the entire curve. Using their knowledge and experience a coach helps you run a strong and impactful race over the course of the entire curve. A coach does something for you that you can't do for yourself—build and support a plan that bridges your current reality with your envisioned future.

## 3. *Practice*

Ray Bradbury, the legendary author, said, "I know you've heard it a thousand times before. But it's true--hard work pays off. If you want to be good, you have to practice, practice, practice.

Practice under the watchful eye of a coach improves the effectiveness and efficiency of your deliberate practice. A coach possesses the specific subject-matter expertise necessary to guide your development—beginning with breaking down your targeted performance improvements into smaller actions and increments that are easier to digest and practice. Then they guide you to perfect the incremental pieces and weave it back together while providing feedback along the way. No one can gift you the key to unlocking your potential. It must be earned and shaped through experience that can only be gained through practice. Yes, there it is again—practice.

A coach supports you through the process of deliberate practice to help you optimize your own individuality, uniqueness and potential.

### 4. *Encourage*

Coaches are encouragers. Coaches push you to overcome your fears and turn doubt into boldness—turning uncertainty into confidence. Encouragement is not opposed to effort. Coaches are not blind optimists telling you what you want to hear. Coaches don't expect a fail-proof pattern of success but encourage you towards an increasing pattern of effectiveness and improvement.

> **Coaches don't expect a fail-proof pattern of success but encourage you towards an increasing pattern of effectiveness and improvement.**

Mike Ditka, the Super Bowl winning coach of the Chicago Bears, is called "Da Coach." A good friend and long time Bears fan of mine told me this story about Ditka's coaching philosophy. A master of motivation and encouragement, Ditka was asked the secret to his coaching success. Ditka said, "It's all about their butts." "What do you mean?" the surprised reporter replied. "You need to know which ones to kiss, which ones to pat, and which ones to kick." Coaches encourage effort and progress that helps you consistently take the next best step.

Ditka is right. How a coach delivers encouragement is essential to raising performance. In fact, a group of researchers from eight leading universities, including Columbia, Stanford and Yale, set out to identify how the delivery of encouragement makes a difference in performance.

The research focused on determining if the way feedback is delivered could lead to improved performance without adversely affecting motivation and self-confidence. When one phrase, containing 19 words, was used, performance rose a minimum of 40%—"I'm giving you these comments because I have very high expectations and I know you can reach them."[12]

Why is this type of encouragement from a coach magical? Because when you receive authentic belief-filled encouragement tied to high expectations, from a coach you trust, it piques your mental and emotional curiosity. Encouragement from a coach eliminates barriers to improvement and leads you to increase your effort and unlock your potential.

### 5. *Equip*

Coaches equip you to run effectively on your own. Regardless of how close your coach may be to your race, they can't step in and run in your place. The real measure of success for a coach is his or her ability to assist you in developing a base of self-awareness, knowledge and expertise that enhances your ability to self-coach.

How did you learn to ride a bike? While you might have employed training wheels, your big breakthrough was most likely credited to a coach. A coach who equipped you by running alongside of you, hand on the seat, until you were able to do it on your own.

Who hasn't performed well in practice only to deliver a poor on-stage performance? Who hasn't practiced perfectly leading up to a performance and froze standing alone under the bright lights? The equipping process improves your ability to make in-game adjustments and use the experience to improve your preparation. This is why you never forget coaches who helped you get comfortable being uncomfortable.

A coach is committed to helping you shine when you are running alone.

## The Rest of the Story

Coaches take you to places you couldn't go on your own. Steve Ridgeway, a former PLU NAIA All-America linebacker said, "Frosty Westering gave me a faith to build my life on; he gave me hope for the future and a sense that love never fails."[13]

In 1999, Pacific Lutheran University moved up in competition from NAIA to NCAA Div. III. The Westering-led Lutes rose to the challenge. They finished the regular season 8-1 and earned a spot in the playoffs. They were the underdogs, but I am sure Frosty was excited for another opportunity to reinforce a powerful life lesson—"A winning attitude constantly accents our strengths rather than our weaknesses, our desires rather than our fears. It's that dynamic spirit in our heart and soul that says, I can, I will, I must, regardless of the odds."

The Lutes won four straight road games on their way to Frosty's eighth appearance in a national championship game. It was a Cinderella story. During the week leading up to the national title game, sportswriters wrote about Frosty's remarkable career—the coach focused on his calling.

Standing between Frosty and his fourth national championship title was Div. III powerhouse Rowan. The Profs were fresh off a semi-final victory over defending champion Mount Union—breaking MU's record 54 game-winning streak, and string of three consecutive national championships.

Few people gave Frosty and his team much of a chance. But they didn't know this game was going to be won with "MAGIC." Frosty wasn't a magician, but he did know how to get the best out of his players when only extraordinary would do—conjure up some "MAGIC"—Make A Greater Individual Commitment."

On December 18, in Salem, Virginia, a focused and committed PLU team defeated Rowan 43-13. Coach Frosty and his team delivered PLU's fourth national football championship. Talking about championships, Frosty said, "A championship, in the world, gives you authenticity that you did it. But that really doesn't say anything until you ask, 'What was the trip like?' The trip was the greatest thing in life, whether we won or lost."[14]

Great coaches prepare you for the race. They help you discover your best so your level of preparation will exceed the requirements of your race. Who's your coach? What do you want your race to be like? The secret to great preparation that positions you for lasting impact is to engage and enlist the support of coaches. You'll win some, and you will lose some, but you'll be prepared to run your best race.

# PART 3

# Go!

## "Running a Great Race"

> *"Our greatest fear should not be of failure but of succeeding at things in life that don't really matter."*
> —FRANCIS CHAN

> *"Get a friend to tell you your faults, or better still, welcome an enemy who will watch you keenly and sting you savagely. What a blessing such an irritating critic will be to a wise man."*
> —CHARLES SPURGEON

> *"There must be a beginning of any great matter, but the continuing unto the end until it be thoroughly finished yields the true glory."*
> —SIR FRANCIS DRAKE

# CHAPTER 10

# Commitment: "Staying in Your Lane"

*"Never trade what you want at the moment for what you want the most."*
—JOHN MAXWELL

*"One cannot collect all the beautiful shells on the beach."*
—ANNE MORROW LINDBERGH

Everything wasn't normal. It was normal for me to be sitting in church on Sunday morning. And we could certainly expect that Pastor Johnson would deliver a solid three-point sermon—he was predictable that way. Most Sundays I paid attention, but this was not a normal Sunday. Billy Graham could have been in the pulpit on this Sunday and I may not have noticed.

I wasn't the only one tuning in and out. There was always something different about church on this particular Sunday morning in May. Glancing around I could see people fiddling to secure earbuds. A plethora of whispers added to the distractions created by kids wrestling over Cheerios. The prayers of the day spoke to what was on our hearts and minds—race day.

On this Sunday the 59th running of the Indianapolis 500 was about to begin. And a member of our church, Tom Sneva, was driving in the race. Tom's riveting and gutsy display of driving in his Indy 500 debut, the prior year, caught the eye of iconic racing team owner Roger Penske. Penske was enamored with Tom's raw talent and signed him to drive for his elite team. Tom Sneva, a former math teacher who grew up in a racing family, was no longer driving in relative obscurity. When they raised the green flag on this Sunday morning, Tom was driving a car capable of winning the granddaddy of auto racing.

Nearly 2,000 miles away, in Indianapolis, Indiana, 300,000 people jammed into the stands and track infield to view this great racing spectacle. Nearly half of the televisions in America tuned in to watch. The cry, "Gentlemen start your engines," readied the racers to prepare for the start of the race.

Sneva started the race in the second row right behind the pole sitter, A. J. Foyt.[1] Tom was driving well and running in the top five as he approached lap 126—74 laps to go. Sneva was running side by side with Indy rookie Eldon Rasmussen as they entered turn two. Sneva, racing on the inside, began to edge ahead of Rasmussen. Those listening to the race instead of the sermon gasped. No one needed to ask what happened—we knew. It was horrible. Tom had crashed.

Working out of the turn, instead of holding his line, Rasmussen moved off his line and dropped down on the curve, catching Sneva's back tire and creating what Keith Jackson called "an incredible accident...a spectacular flip." The car, now airborne, flipped into the wall, instantly splitting it in half. The impact set off a fiery explosion.

The cockpit of Tom's car flipped twice, with Sneva still aboard, catapulting it down the track before it came spinning to rest on the track. In shocking disbelief, racing great Jackie Stewart said, "This is one of the most horrifying crashes I have ever seen."[2] Tom can be seen struggling mightily to extract himself from the cockpit. Safety crews arrived on the scene and worked urgently to extinguish the fire that burned 15% of Tom's body.

A few months later Tom spoke to my high school church group about his faith and experience at Indianapolis that fateful day in 1975. What happened? With only 74 laps to go and a chance to win the Indy 500, how could such a tragic mistake occur? Tom had done his homework—every professional driver does. Homework means studying the behaviors and driving tendencies of every driver in the race so they can anticipate what to expect when driving in traffic with them. Eldon Rasmussen was a rookie so there was not a lot of knowledge about him. But Tom and

Eldon had practiced driving through turn two together, in practice, more than once.

During practice, Eldon consistently held the line of his car through the turn. Tom expected him to do the same as they sped side by side into turn two on race day. But this time Eldon didn't hold his line. He got distracted by the moment—maybe the traffic, speed or adrenaline caused him to do the unexpected. A momentary lapse of focus and commitment resulted in one of the most spectacular crashes in Indy 500 racing history.

If Eldon Rasmussen had stayed in his lane, Tom Sneva may have won the biggest race of his professional life. Instead, it demonstrates a valuable lesson. To maximize your opportunity for personal and professional impact, you have to stay in your lane! It is your race. Everyone has been assigned a unique lane reflecting their roles, values and goals. Your individual lane leads to the finish line you have defined, described, and clarified.

### It's your lane

There is incredible beauty and rich impact in your lane. Your lane has no traffic and no speed limit. Anytime you drive on a freeway you recognize that people do not like staying in a single lane or driving the speed limit. If traffic starts to slow in your lane, you begin to check out the adjoining lanes, looking to shift to a faster moving lane. You see the car in the adjoining lane edge a few hundred feet ahead and pick up speed. It's a sure invitation to put your blinker on and work your way over to the faster lane.

If you've driven in Southern California or any large metropolitan area, you know exactly what I am talking about. You take pride in finding the fast lane. But not for long. You glance back to the lane you just left. Now it is beginning to move. What do you do? Of course you put yourself in harm's way again. You dodge the lane-splitting motorcyclists and move over just in time for that lane to put on the brakes.

Staying in your lane creates the strategic racing advantage of focus. Focusing on your lane is where you most effectively use your time, talent, and energy on maximizing your contribution to the lives of the people you want to impact most. Making and retaining your commitment to stay in your lane is challenging. All it takes is an innocent glance over to see other lanes moving faster and you begin to doubt you are in the right lane. You lose focus and commitment wanes—without noticing you fall out of your lane.

## What Will You Do When the Race Gets Tough?

Dr. Viktor Frankl spent three life-threatening years at Auschwitz at the hands of the Nazis during World War II. He talked about his experience and learnings in his book, *Man's Search for Meaning*. I've read this book several times through the years. The pages are yellowed and the many highlights faded. But Dr. Frankl's words still jump off the page for anyone serious about learning how to run an impactful race.

Frankl's frightening experience led him to a vital discovery about impact. Frankl wrote,

"We who lived in concentration camps can remember the men who walked through the huts comforting others, giving away their last piece of bread. They may have been few in number, but they offer sufficient proof that everything can be taken from a man but one thing: the last of human freedoms—to choose one's attitude in any given set of circumstance, to choose one's own way.

And there are always choices to make. Every day, every hour, offered the opportunity to make a decision, a decision which determined whether you would or would not submit to those powers which threatened to rob you of your very self, your inner freedom, which determined whether or not you would become the plaything of circumstance, renouncing freedom and dignity to become molded into the form of the typical inmate.

Even though conditions such as lack of sleep, insufficient food and various mental stress may suggest that the inmates were bound to react in certain ways, in the final analysis it becomes clear that the sort of person the prisoner became was the result of an inner decision and not the result of camp influences alone. Fundamentally, therefore, any man can, even under such circumstances, decide what shall become of him—mentally and spiritually."[3]

Few if any of us will face the circumstances and conditions described by Dr. Frankl. His experience provides firsthand insight into the power your choices have on how well you will run your race. As Frankl points out, "There are always choices to make. Every day, every hour, offered the opportunity to make a decision..."[4]

## What Does Staying in Your Lane Mean?

The decision to stay in your lane is tough when you are constantly bombarded with distracting alternatives. Staying in your lane is the decision to remain steadfastly committed to the development of your most important roles. Running in your lane, you will be able to create life-changing impact by intentionally and purposefully living your roles out.

There is something about our volitional nature that is both empowering and dangerous. Why is it we can declare our allegiance to what we know to be important and yet lose focus so easily? Dr. Barry Schwartz, author of *The Paradox of Choice*, says, "...choice improves the quality of our lives. It enables us to control our destinies and to come close to getting what we want out of any situation...we would be better off if we paid less attention to what others around us were doing."[5]

You can't stay in your lane, focused on the roles that truly matter to you, if you are constantly looking around to see what others are doing. Dr. Schwartz points out that it is the difference between being a "chooser" versus a "picker." "'Choosers' are active: they interrogate their own goals and critically evaluate how well the various options enable them to meet those goals. Choosing is work; it takes time, attention, and effort. But it bears fruit: real depth of involvement with the options."[6] "Choosers" don't let what is going on around them become a distraction—they avoid getting pulled into another lane.

The alternative is "picking." "'Picking' is much more passive. You lie on your couch as options come by on a metaphorical conveyor belt, and you pick one that appeals to you. Pickers won't be interrogating their goals. They won't be saying 'none of the above' to the options they are presented with. We are all pickers some of the time, when, for example, after a hard day of work, we flop on the couch and channel surf until we find something tolerable to watch. When we're feeling exhausted in this way, we won't turn off the TV if nothing decent is on and read a book. My fear is that overwhelming options turns all of us into pickers, at least much of the time."[7]

"Pickers" consistently waste their time, talent and resources. You must actively and consciously take your thoughts captive in order to be a "chooser." You cannot allow your thoughts to be hijacked by life's buffet of countless options. Staying in your lane means staying focused on your most important races and not being lured into running races that don't really matter.

> You cannot allow your thoughts to be hijacked by life's buffet of countless options.

## What Will it Take to Stay in Your Lane?

What's the first thing that comes to your mind when you hear the word *discipline*? Whatever came to your mind I am confident it wasn't *celebration*. When I was 13, I had my heart set on owning a brand new Schwinn 10-speed bike. It was an expensive bike—$99.99 before tax (equivalent to $570.13 in 2015). They never went on sale, and I was told I would have to buy it with my own money. To earn the money, I accepted a job delivering an advertising circular to 500 homes a week. I would earn $.005 for each home on the route, or the princely sum of $2.50 a week.

I calculated it would take me 42 weeks to earn enough to buy the bike. I did not calculate that it would take three to four hours, every Wednesday, to get the work done. About half way through the third week of deliveries, I decided I was going to quit—too hard for so little pay. At dinner I announced, "I am quitting my circular route." I was expecting my dad to push back, but he didn't say a word. Later he came into my room and told me it was my decision, but I couldn't quit until my manager could find a replacement. Walking out of my room he asked, "What color did you pick for your new bike?"

I wanted to quit, but my dad knew I wanted the bike more although I am confident he still wouldn't have let me quit before my manager found a replacement. I eventually bought the bike and retired from delivering circulars. More importantly I learned an invaluable lesson—celebration follows discipline.

I don't think we ever make friends with discipline. We enjoy a strained relationship with it at best. But, if you want to celebrate winning great races, it can't be done without discipline. Commitment grows out of adherence to discipline.

Discipline keeps you from wandering away from your intended and desired race into another lane. Discipline is not something anyone can impose on you. They can only create opportunities for you to discover it within yourself. Great finishes ultimately reflect the consistent commitment to take defined and decisive action even when you don't feel like doing it and the odds seem to be stacked against you.

> **Great finishes ultimately reflect the consistent commitment to take defined and decisive action even when you don't feel like doing it and the odds seem to be stacked against you.**

## A picture of commitment

I was locked into my career when Walt encouraged me to give up safety and security. I was progressing nicely, working a salary-plus-bonus sales position, when Walt challenged me to consider the unlimited income potential of full-commission sales with his company. While clinging to safety, hearing I could earn five to twenty times what I was earning at the time piqued more than passing curiosity. Interested in learning more, I asked Walt if I could spend a day with him observing and asking questions.

My first question, "What time shall I meet you?" was greeted with a surprising answer. Instantly he replied, "six o'clock." "In the morning?" I thought. I immediately knew there was something different about how Walt approached his work. The next morning Walt was waiting for me when I pulled up. I jumped in his car, and for nearly 10 hours, I witnessed flawless attention to detail and precise execution. There was a reason for everything Walt did right down to wiping his shoes with a shine cloth before he walked in to meet a customer.

Walt was committed to his role as a sales professional—he stayed in his lane. He consistently did what others were unwilling to do. Walt consistently produced exceptional results and earned an extraordinary income. I was always surprised when people would ask me to describe what made Walt successful. I used these words from Henry Wadsworth Longfellow to describe Walt at a sales awards dinner, "The heights of great men reached and kept were not obtained by sudden flight; but they, while their companions slept, were toiling upward in the night."[8]

Walt performed like a perfectly-scripted advertisement. It ran every day at the same time, with the same message. Walt exercised an ongoing pattern of disciplined actions. He relentlessly committed to staying in his lane. Walt would not allow himself to take his eyes off his goals and be distracted by what was going on in other lanes.

## Keep Your Eyes on Your Lane

The Urban Dictionary can be a source of edgy and pointed wisdom. It defined "staying in your lane" as "mind your own business, keep moving straight ahead..."[9] Good advice if you're going to deliver life-changing impact. Thomas Edison, the great scientist and inventor, said, "Many of life's failures are men who did not realize how close they were to success when they gave up." Neil Baldwin, author of *Edison, Inventing the Century*, writes, "Edison's career was an example of supreme synergy, four decades before that word was even created."[10] Thomas Edison forged great discovery and contribution by staying in his lane.

While leading a multilocation distribution business with nearly one billion dollars in revenue, my teams faced waves of difficult and demanding facility and systems projects. The precision and coordination demanded by the work was taking a physical, intellectual and emotion toll on everyone. Tempers were getting short—nerves were frayed.

Completing the project was dependent upon team members trusting each other to do their job—to stay in their lane. Tangible progress was not always visible to every team member, which added to their frustration. Highlighting the importance of staying committed to your lane, I kicked off our monthly leadership meeting with a question, "How long does it take for a bamboo tree to grow?" I looked out into a sea of blank stares and rolling eyes. I am sure more than one of them was thinking, "Really, Jim! We are in the midst of chaos and you want to talk about how to grow bamboo trees?"

I explained to them that it takes over five years for a bamboo tree to mature. In the first four years the soil where the seed is planted is nurtured with water and fertilizer but will show no signs of growth. In the fifth year a tiny sprout breaks through the earth. Amazingly, in less than six months it shoots up over 100 feet. What was not visible to the naked eye was setting the stage for spectacular growth.

The bamboo farmer was staying in his lane knowing his work was not in vain. While the seed was not showing signs of growth, the disciplined cultivation of the soil was nurturing a root system capable of supporting the tremendous growth and height of the tree—the result of commitment. The field tenders stayed in their lane, understanding the potential in the seeds they planted.

High-level commitment is most difficult to maintain when you don't feel like you are making progress or your effort is not being rewarded. Ultimately our team did an exceptional job of executing the plan. In the weeks following our meeting I saw the story of the bamboo tree pinned on bulletin boards and posted in cubicles and offices across our 21 facilities. People were using it as a reminder to stay in their lane and remain committed to excellence in their assignments.

### The truth about planting seeds

The power of this story is grounded in two important truths. First, you must choose the right seed to plant. Persistence is only valuable if it is directed toward a specific and well-defined finish line. In the case of our business it was a well-thought-out strategy that was going to improve our business performance. In your case it is defining the lanes for your race based on selecting roles, values and goals that provide you with the best opportunity for lasting and sustained impact.

One evening my wife and I were having dinner with a young woman we have known since birth. We were celebrating her upcoming wedding and meeting her fiancé. We reminisced about her mom, who passed away two years earlier. It was amazing how much she now reminded us of all of her mom's wonderful qualities. Hearing that comparison, she lamented how much trouble she had caused her mother during her teenage years.

Now, just weeks before her wedding, she was going through her mom's possessions. She laughed about clothes with tags still hanging on them and shoes that had never been worn. But she paused to collect herself before telling us about finding one of her mom's journals. "I began to page through it. I couldn't understand how important this was back then," she said. What she discovered page after page was the power and impact of staying committed to your lane. One page after the other her mom had scribbled a single large entry across the page, "I love you even when you say you hate me."

> You have critical roles that consistently and profoundly touch the lives of the people you love—even when they don't love you back.

You have critical roles that consistently and profoundly touch the lives of the people you love—even when they don't love you back. You must persist in cultivating these roles even knowing you may never see the seeds of your vision fulfilled.

The second truth is that you will plant the wrong seed from time to time. If you are pursuing the wrong strategy, a change may be in order. If you are investing in the wrong roles, selecting ineffective goals or ignoring the truth in your results, you need to reevaluate. Discipline born out of persistent pursuit of the wrong finish lines is a waste of time. George Bernard Shaw, the only person to be awarded a Nobel Prize and an Academy Award, said, "Progress is impossible without change, and those who cannot change their minds cannot change anything."

Isn't being right so much easier than admitting we were wrong? It's hard to make a change if we are heavily invested in a decision that carries significant responsibility or commitment. But show me someone who has led a life of perpetual and sustained victory and success and I'll show you someone who has lived below their potential.

In her book *Pathfinders*, Gail Sheehy explores the qualities possessed by people who are able to overcome difficulty and setbacks. Sheehy writes, "Although it is difficult to believe, great men and women often feel helpless and afraid...It is the rare leader who at some point in life does not become convinced that he or she has failed."[11]

Staying in your lane is not a mistake-free, failure-proof racing strategy. You are not always going to choose the right fork in the road. You will find yourself needing to make changes from time to time. Remember your races run over the pattern of the sigmoid curve—races have cycles and seasons. As your roles change and evolve, you'll occasionally need to make adjustments. "Everything—including relationships—tends to deteriorate with time unless the new, the improved, the changed is added."[12]

> Show me someone who has led a life of perpetual and sustained victory and success and I'll show you someone who has lived below their potential.

## How To Stay in Your Lane

Choosing your lane is hard work; it takes time, attention and effort not to drift away from your most valuable races. If you want your race to become a reflection of your most important roles and highest goals, you must commit to staying in your lane. You can't run someone else's race, and they cannot run yours.

If you've eaten at an In-N-Out Burger, you never forget the experience. They have built a cult following by being clear about who they are as a company and staying in their lane. Harry Snyder, co-founder, sums up what it means to stay in your lane when he said, "Keep it real simple. Do one thing and do it the best you can."[13] Regardless of what their competitors did with their menus and stores, In-N-Out Burger kept it simple. They didn't turn their stores into playgrounds and they have not changed their menu since Harry Truman was President of the United States. That would be 1948 for those of you counting backwards.

Burgers, fries, milkshakes and drinks—simple clarity. You can mix up the ingredients, order them in different combinations and add a few twists to their traditional ingredients if you know the secret menu. But when you look at the menu the choices are simple. When you walk into In-N-Out Burger, you know exactly what to expect.

If someone was describing your race today, how would they describe it? Are you the same person publicly, privately and personally? The heart of staying in your lane is grounded in the clarity and alignment of your roles, values, and goals. The people you most want to impact need to know exactly what to expect from you. There is a reason why in Solomon's wisdom he said, "Where there is no vision, the people perish."[14]

Remember your lane is all yours—no traffic and no speed limit. The best way to run faster and create greater impact begins with carefully defining your roles, values and goals—then holding tightly to them. An effective way to review your race status and renew your commitment to running in your lane is to ask yourself three questions.

## Lane-defining questions

1. What do you need to do more of?
2. What do you need to do less of?
3. What do you need to stop doing?

Will it matter? The power of these questions lies in the fact that this is not an assignment or a project—these questions help you establish guardrails to keep you in your lane. Your goal is to identify and focus on the actions and behaviors capable of producing life-changing and life-sustaining impact on the most important people in your life.

> "There is only one time that is important—now! It is the most important time because it the only time we have any power over."
> —Leo Tolstoy

Leo Tolstoy wrote, "There is only one time that is important—now! It is the most important time because it the only time we have any power over." I know this is important because, according to The Energy Project, 58% of us say there is a significant gap between what we say is important in our lives and how we actually live our lives. The research goes on to say that 69% of us have a hard time focusing, are easily distracted during the day, and take too little time for the activities we enjoy most.[15]

Think about what this means for a moment. The majority of people are spending their time, talent, and resources running the wrong races—in spite of what they say is important to them. No one has to tell you what the problem is. You know that on most days your responsibilities, to-do list and ambitions exceed what you can get done. By applying these three lane-defining questions, you will build personal barriers that will keep you from migrating towards doing what is easy, comfortable and habitual.

Abraham Maslow in his book, *The Farther Reaches of Human Nature*, says we evade growth. Maslow labeled the defense to growth as "the fear of one's own greatness, the evasion of one's destiny, or the running away from one's best talent." He went on to conclude, "If you deliberately plan to be less than you are capable of being, then I warn you that you'll be deeply unhappy for the rest of your life. You'll be evading your own capacities, your own possibilities."[10]

It is not only a matter of saying "yes" to what is most important, it requires you to say "no." Saying "no" will ultimately become your most important ally to your commitment to stay in your lane. Don't waste your time doing things that don't matter. Think about it this way—if you can't identify what doesn't matter, you are wasting your time. If you frequently ask these questions, you will begin to identify what to leave undone.

Think of your lane as your calling. Paulo Coelho, the gifted writer of *The Alchemist*, writes, "We all need to be aware of our personal calling. What is a personal calling? It is God's blessing, it is the path that God chose for you here on Earth."

> "We all need to be aware of our personal calling. What is a personal calling? It is God's blessing, it is the path that God chose for you here on Earth."
> —Paulo Coelho

The race you have been called to run matters. Staying in your lane provides you with the greatest opportunity to experience moments of grandeur, joy, contribution and learning because in your lane lies the greatest opportunity for impact. You will come to a point in your race when only you can decide whether you are going to stay in your lane. You will need to make a choice. Do you really want what awaits you at the finish line? Are you really committed to making an impact? Life will present you with options, but it is up to you to choose to stay in your lane.

# CHAPTER 11

# Accountability: "Never Run Alone"

> *"Be thoroughly acquainted with your temptations and the things that may corrupt you, especially those temptations that either your company or your business will lay before you."*
> —RICHARD BAXTER

> *"Behavior that is observed changes."*
> —BRUCE LARSON

What happened? It is almost unthinkable that anyone could fall so fast. How could they be in the midst of running admired and celebrated races and run right off a cliff. Who plans on being broken or defeated before crossing the finish line?—they didn't; no one does. But when you run alone, danger lurks everywhere.

Who am I talking about? I am sure you can fill in the ___*blank*___ with a name. There are plenty of options. Lance Armstrong, a multiple Tour de France winner and cancer survivor. Tiger Woods, former number one golfer in the world and an iconic personal brand. Kenneth Lay and Jeffrey Skilling, prominent corporate leaders who led Enron Corporation into scandalous bankruptcy. Political history is littered with race failures—Richard Nixon resigned the presidency of the United States. John Edwards was once a promising presidential candidate. And five Senators who became known as the Keating Five after their missteps contributed to the savings and loan collapse in the late 1980's.

It is very hard to finish strong. There are so many potential pitfalls along the way. B. C. Forbes said, "How you start is important, very important, but in the end it is how you finish that counts. It is easier to be a self-starter than a self-finisher. The victor in the race is not the one who dashes off swiftest but the one who leads at the finish."

Getting started is easy. Then in the midst of the race you begin to experience trials. Challenges rise and you give in to the resistance. Self-finishing is a lonely journey. Running alone is difficult and a potentially fatal race strategy. Self-finishers pride themselves on self-reliance and independence, resulting in the unintended introduction of danger and peril.

Independence is filled with good intentions, but it will not result in a race that creates the impact you desire. To reach the finish line you desire and to celebrate lasting impact on the people you love, the teams you lead and the causes that stir your heart, don't run alone.

Solomon shared the wisdom of accountability when he said, "Two are better than one, because they have a good return for their labor: If either of them falls down, one can help the other up. But pity anyone who falls and has no one to help them up."[1]

## We Pride Ourselves on Being Independent

Experience in life is inevitable—it just happens whether we invite it or not. But, unfortunately, learning from our experiences is optional. Whether from our own experience or the observable experiences of others, we are not precluded from repeating poor decisions, failing to do what is required or repeating failed history. The path to personal independence is paved with excitement and lined with danger. Filled with anxious anticipation, we run towards perceived freedom with unabated enthusiasm.

Who hasn't welcomed the thought of being all grown up?—relishing the freedom to choose your own path and make your own decisions. J. Martin Kohe, author of *Your Greatest Power*, writes, "Any person who recognizes this greatest power... the power to choose... begins to realize that he is the one that is doing the choosing and that friends, although they mean well, cannot do his choosing for him, nor can his relatives. Consequently, he develops real self-confidence based upon his own ability, upon his own action, and upon his own initiative."[2]

If you grew up in a relatively stable home environment, you understood that your every move was constantly on display. You likely bemoaned the lack of privacy and the adherence to rules. You may have even proclaimed on more than one occasion, "I can hardly wait to be on my own."

Weren't we all smarter than our parents when we were teenagers? On some level we most certainly thought we were. I don't remember having a precise curfew growing up, but I know I left the house many times being told what time I needed to be home. My mom consistently said, "If you are out after midnight, you are up to nothing but no good." How did she know? You don't have to think too long about this to see the truth in this statement.

On our way out the door we think "free at last." We quickly run towards this glamorous perception of independence that we have concocted in our minds. All we know is it's going to be great. Hello, world! Remember the description of the discovery phase of a race—dumb and happy? We step away from a structured and supportive environment to one filled with an overabundance of privacy and freedom. Chuck Swindoll describes the gateway to early independence this way, "Too many hours of independence easily leads to a fall—ethically or morally, financially or spiritually...Without the safety net of checks and balances, a fall can be not only far but fatal."[3]

> "Too many hours of independence easily leads to a fall—ethically or morally, financially or spiritually... Without the safety net of checks and balances, a fall can be not only far but fatal."
> —Chuck Swindoll

## The List No One Gets to See

Ah, dumb and happy, with moments of dumb and dumber thrown in. As I prepared to speak to a men's group about impact and accountability, I thought about my personal path to independence. Wow, I did some dumb stuff—really dumb stuff. Who hasn't, right?

As the years pass, hopefully our dumb becomes funny. As I opened my talk I told the group some of the dumb stuff. It is now funny to tell people about going to the golf course the morning after my second son was born. A bold move no doubt wrapped in stupidity. How do you respond when your wife calls and asks, "Where are you?" "Hmm, just a second. Can I call you back?" would have at least given me a chance to think of how to explain being dumb.

After they laughed about my account of dumb and dumber, I shifted gears. I told them I was going to share the ten things I was most ashamed of in my life. You know, the shameful and embarrassing experiences of life you have locked away in the distant recesses of your mind. Things you know would have likely never happened in the light of accountability. The mere mention of unlocking the door to my personal vault of dumb and painful certainly grabbed everyone's attention. If anyone had not been paying attention they were now—all eyes were on me.

I paused briefly. I slowly panned my audience, ensuring that I made eye contact with every man in the room. Then I said, "After I share my top ten list, let's all share in the fun. In the spirit of authentic disclosure we will go around the room and each of you will get a chance to share something from your top ten list of painful moments." Immediately the body language in the room was transformed. Everyone slumped down in their chairs as if I had flipped on a switch. Eyes began to roam about the room. I tried to make eye contact, but no one wanted to risk eye contact because it might suggest they were willing participants.

Their response was exactly what I expected. The stage was set to make an important point. "How many of you value independence?" I asked. It was obviously an easy question because hands rose and heads nodded agreement. Who doesn't want to be in control?

We value and covet independence above most things—especially accountability. Let's be honest...we admire independence. Flying solo is popular. Independence was near the top of my list when I was interviewing job candidates—critical for sales roles. It's hard to imagine that someone could be successful in sales without valuing independence. Most placed significant value on their independence.

However, when we worked with our sales team on skill improvement, we would commonly hear, "Why do I have to do all of this? If I am getting the results, just leave me alone and let me do my job." But there was something missing. Independent ambition alone was not enough. Year after year salespeople who overvalued independence were our most inconsistent performers. They followed a pattern of a year of stellar performance scattered amongst prolonged mediocrity. Running alone, they resisted what they needed most to generate consistent and reliable performance—accountability.

The problem that self-finishing independence presents and entrenches is pride. Pride creates barriers to progress—not allowing you to ask for help. Pride clouds perception and falsely leads you to believe you'll appear weak. Independence without accountability leads to isolation. Once you isolate yourself, all you can draw upon is your own strength, resources and talent—a perfect recipe for failure.

## The Full-Meal Deal

> If feedback is breakfast, accountability is the full-meal deal.

Accountability is what everyone needs and no one wants. Ken Blanchard, the best-selling author and management consultant, says, "Feedback is the breakfast of champions." If feedback is breakfast, accountability is the full-meal deal. Accountability is the essential ingredient for running with perseverance and finishing strong.

Accountability means opening yourself up to review—facing tough questions and listening rather than defending. Accountability drives performance improvement, but most importantly it will keep you from screwing up. Randy Pausch, author of *The Last Lecture*, wrote, "When you're screwing up and nobody says anything to you anymore, that means they've given up on you...When you see yourself doing something badly and nobody's bothering to tell you anymore, that's a bad place to be."[4]

I am confident that no one embarking on an important race dreams of screwing it up, but it happens all the time. Think about decisions that took you off course while running your races. What are the chances of running off course if someone had been running alongside of you, holding you accountable?

## Your meal is served

My youngest son, Andrew, is fiercely independent. You might say he is stubborn, but fiercely independent sounds better. When he went off to college, he strongly claimed his independence. He placed my wife and me on an "as needs to know basis." Known to many parents as: "I will call you when I need something. Don't expect any personal news. I'll save up the social conversation for holidays."

Out to lunch on a Sunday, with my wife and family, my phone rang. I looked down to see Andrew was calling. I quickly excused myself from the table, knowing this was not a call to check in on how Mom and Dad were doing. While a variety of scenarios raced through my mind, I answered as if he called to tell me he missed me. "Hey Andrew, how are you doing?" Then I braced myself for what was coming next.

Andrew didn't even hear me ask how he was! He immediately responded, "I have something to tell you." I zero in on his condition again, "Are you alright?" I ask. Always a young man of few words and little emotion, he replies, "Yes, we had a party at the house last night. The police showed up." I am now facing an overwhelming dilemma. Do I launch into my interrogation and lecture, reminding him that experience is inevitable but learning is optional?—my not so subtle way of reminding him to pay attention means anticipating bad outcomes? Or do I bite my tongue because he appears to be on the path of accountability?

I bit my tongue—hard! I was challenged not to jump into lecture mode. Especially when I heard the police were returning on Tuesday. "Returning for what?" I asked. Well, it was their second noise complaint. If they received a formal citation, it would require a court appearance. Ah, now I know why he is calling. He has come to the end of the independence road. There is no shelter from a court appearance. "Now is the time for the *experience is inevitable, learning is optional* reminder," I thought.

Who hasn't been in the midst of a situation, of your own making, and realized the potential gravity of the circumstances?—a moment when you wish you could turn back time and choose differently. Even wondering why someone didn't point out the looming danger, only to be reminded you were warned—many times. When you run head first into accountability, you learn a lot about yourself.

Four of Andrew's seven roommates chose not to attend the meeting with the police—they opted for independence over accountability. The police respected the way Andrew handled the situation and did not issue a citation. He received a powerful lesson in accountability. I was proud of Andrew. It brought a smile to my face to realize he had been paying attention.

> **Performance rises in the light of accountability because it shuns indecision and complacency.**

Wouldn't it be so much easier if accountability could be discovered in private? Who likes to live out the responsibility of fulfilling commitments where others can see they have been met?—anyone who wants to improve performance and expand their influence. Performance rises in the light of accountability because it shuns indecision and complacency. Accountability surrounds your race with the strength, support and encouragement necessary for you to increase your impact.

## You Are Going to Be Held Accountable

Who hasn't heard these words, "You are going to be held accountable." What do you think of when you hear these words? Don't images of great rewards and benefits start dancing through your head? Of course not. You more likely sensed impending punishment and negative consequences. Interestingly enough regardless of your perception, you are going to be held accountable.

Billy Graham was identified among the 10 most admired men in the world for the 58th time in Gallup's 2014 survey...the most appearances by any man in the world since Gallup started the survey...27 more times than former President Ronald Reagan.[5]

Graham's path to admiration emerged out of an important meeting he held with his team in 1948, in Modesto, California. Graham's leadership team gathered to map out plans for the next 50 years. Billy's team had regularly discussed "the poor image so-called mass evangelism had in the eyes of many people." At this meeting they identified four things that had led to the failure of men who had run the race before Billy: "shady handling of money, sexual immorality, badmouthing others doing similar work, and exaggerated accomplishments."

From this work came what they called the "Modesto Manifesto." "Billy's team structured the ministry to reinforce guidelines and hold themselves accountable...To ratchet up accountability, Graham formed a board of significant leaders, gave that board authority, and accepted supervision."[6]

Billy Graham is one of the most admired and influential men in modern history. He knew he was going to be held accountable. High stakes with significant opportunities for impact are the nature of purpose-filled races. The history of men and women who rose to influence and impact is littered with failure. Billy Graham didn't break the failure code. He simply embraced it. He surrounded himself with accountability—he did not run alone.

Accountability does not yield perfection. It acknowledges our imperfections. Mohandas Gandhi captures the essence of accountability, saying, "There is no one without faults not even men of God. They are men of God, not because they are faultless but because they know their own faults, they strive against them, they do not hide them and are ever ready to correct themselves."[7]

> **Accountability does not yield perfection. It acknowledges our imperfections.**

## The Benefits of Accountability

Stephen Covey, best selling author of *The 7 Habits of Highly Effective People*, says, "Accountability breeds response-ability." The pursuit of impact is not an easy race to run. The minute you publicly declare your intent to run with purpose you invite resistance. It will show up unexpectedly like an uninvited guest. Resistance pulls your attention away from your most important races. It sends you on detours, slows you down and obscures your view of the finish line. Accountability beats back resistance by equipping you to respond effectively.

When you model and build accountability into your race, you will enjoy benefits that cannot be harvested when you run alone. It is easy to gloss over the significant value of accountability because we see it infringing on our independence. But you are just not sure you want to invite someone alongside you to ask, "How is it going?" How many times in the midst of real need have we been asked this question by a trusted friend and deflected the invitation of help by responding, "Great, thanks."

Even when you know running with an accountability partner will increase your impact, you are still likely to lean towards independence. Accountability feels restrictive and personally dangerous. You think, "What could I possibly gain from someone seeing the gaps between who I really am and who I am striving to become?" Accountability exposes a part of us we would prefer to keep hidden.

Raising your level of accountability is a small price to pay for a plethora of enduring benefits you will enjoy. Accountability will forever change the quality and complexion of your race. Accountability assures that you are surrounded with the people, tools and resources to run and finish the impactful races in your life.

## *Four Benefits of Accountability*

- *Improves your decision making*—The root of nearly every personal failure is a flawed decision-making process. When you are sharing your thought process with someone who is familiar with your roles, values and goals, you are less likely to make a decision that will compromise your race priorities.
- *Sharpens your focus*—Bringing someone along side who simply asks you how you are doing will command your attention. The act of contemplating how you are doing with regard to your stated priorities brings distractions and low-value actions into view. When you report progress on a regular basis, you will more consistently align your time with your most important roles and goals.
- *Raises engagement and improves performance*—"You fall into one of three categories. You know you are winning. You know you are

losing. You don't know the score."[8] My friend Chuck Coonradt regularly proved this to me by helping us create and establish performance scorecards for every job in our business. Accountability leads you to consistently measure progress and improvement that is the basis for improving performance.

- *Promotes new races*—You won't languish in celebrating the achievement of milestone goals. The challenge to sustaining progress over the course of a race is the tendency to relax or coast after winning a victory or achieving a goal. It is this nature to relax or ease up when things are going well that kills momentum. We blindly approach a period of decline and fail to start new races (a new curve). In the absence of accountability you can languish in the past. You need someone to challenge you to start new races.

## Empirical Evidence for Accountability

Dr. Gail Matthews, a psychology professor at Dominican University of California, conducted a "study on how goal achievement in the workplace is influenced by writing goals, committing to goal-directed actions, and accountability for those actions."

The original intent of the study was to determine if constructing specific written goals produced greater goal achievement than either unwritten or nonspecific goals. Participants ranging in age from 23 to 72 were randomly assigned to one of five groups and were given specific instructions to guide them over the course of four weeks.

"Participants pursued a variety of goals including (in order of frequency reported) completing a project, increasing income, increasing productivity, getting organized, enhancing performance/achievement, enhancing life balance, reducing work anxiety and learning a new skill."

Each group was provided a different set of instructions to follow over the course of the study.

- Group 1 participants were asked to simply think about their goals and rate them based on difficulty, importance, extent to which they had the skills and resources to accomplish the goal, their commitment and motivation, and whether they had pursued the goal before.

- Groups 2-5 participants wrote their goals down along with rating on the same dimensions as Group 1.
- Group 3 participants added action steps to their goals.
- Group 4 participants were asked to share their commitments with a friend in addition to constructing written goals with action plans.
- Group 5 participants were asked to send a progress report to a friend on a weekly basis. Participants in this group were also sent weekly reminders to email their progress reports to a friend.

Dr. Matthews' research concluded, "The positive effect of account-ability was supported: those who shared weekly progress reports with a friend accomplished significantly more than those who had unwritten goals, wrote their goals, formulated action commitments or sent those action commitments to a friend." The participants in Group 5 achieved 76% of their goals compared to 43% for Group 1 and 64% for Group 4.[9]

The simple act of accountability by way of sharing progress with a friend significantly raised goal achievement.

## The Mindset of Accountability

Running a poor race does not happen in a moment. It results from a series of bobbles that turn from exception to become the norm. You get out of your lane and change course. You may not have seen it coming. We never do. It just seems to happen.

You're running along and no one steps in to question or challenge what you are doing. Either no one is noticing or no one cares, so it must not be a big deal—right? You slip in keeping your promises to your spouse or kids, stop going to a class, fall off your exercise program or miss deadlines and assignments at work. You spend more time with people and in roles that do not reflect your stated priorities. How did this happen?

It wasn't intentional. But if running a great race and finishing strong were only a matter of our intentions, the race would be easy. Intention becomes resolve when we incorporate accountability. Remember that at this point in our journey together I am building on the foundation laid in previous chapters. You are now running the race. You have already defined your success that includes your most important roles, values and goals. You have a vision for the impact that you are trying to create and defining a successful finish to your race.

Accountability keeps your intentions aligned with your actions. To incorporate it, you need the right mindset. Let's be honest... accountability requires a level of personal disclosure that is difficult—even gut wrenching. We don't like to talk about the flaws and weaknesses we work so hard to mask. In the

> Accountability keeps your intentions aligned with your actions.

light of accountability there is no longer any place to hide poor decisions.

I've nearly melted when someone has had the courageous accountability conversation with me. Even when I have invited honest feedback, knowing I needed to change something, it seemed much worse when I heard it out loud. But it helped me stay on track and run with greater impact.

I know your goal is to be different. Your desire is to build momentum in your race so you can increase your impact on the people you love, the teams you lead and the causes that stir your heart. Billy Graham said, "Man has two great spiritual needs. One is for forgiveness, the other is for goodness." The pathway to fill those needs is building the mindset of accountability.

## Qualities of Accountability

Accountability is a discipline. "A discipline is an activity in our power, which we pursue in order to become able to do what we cannot do by direct effort."[10] A measure of the discipline of accountability is reflected in four qualities.

1. *Honesty*—a commitment to the truth. This is tough because the truth can hurt. The truth can also be painful and even embarrassing.
2. *Ownership*—acknowledgement that conditions and circumstances are not permanent. Responsibility for building, executing and adjusting your race plan to deliver the greatest possible impact.
3. *Willingness*—an open and teachable heart. An invitation to someone to come alongside you, ask the tough questions and point out the gaps between where you are heading and your finish line.

4. _Humility_—an antidote to pride. Pride is stubborn and keeps us from hearing the truth and seeing our flaws. Blinded by pride, we can hurt others and not recognize that we are inflicting pain and damage. A humble spirit opens the door for forgiveness and our ears to hear feedback.[11]

When I read through this list, it stings. It strips away pretense and intention and strikes at your heart. But I think that is why it is called accountability. The nature and effectiveness of accountability must bring us to look at ourselves in ways we can't on our own.

One of the first people I hired in my career turned into a great friend. Jim was easy to work with. His optimism and enthusiasm were contagious. Jim and I worked hand in hand for years, developing a meaningful and trusting work relationship and personal friendship. At one point in our careers, Jim was in a role supporting a business I was running. There were some challenges along the way and I became critical of Jim's work—very critical.

My boss, at the time, was close to both of us. One day, when I was meeting with Pete, he pointed out to me that my relationship with Jim was hurting and it was up to me to fix it. Pete listened patiently as I resisted his counsel and offered support for my behavior and a critique of Jim's performance. Then Pete, gracefully and professionally as he always did, shined the light back on me.

One by one he pointed out my lack of accountability. It was painful, but I was screwing up. I was thankful Pete took the time and had the interest to come alongside of me and get my race back on track. Jim passed away a couple years ago after a long and courageous battle. In the absence of accountability, I would have never been able to support my friend when he needed me most.

## Engaging Accountability

Accountability is paradoxical—its power is derived out of weakness. You look over the qualities of accountability and can quickly conclude you'll pass. But accountability is not an open invitation for anyone to critique you. It is an invitation for someone to join you who cares deeply about helping you run a great race.

Bill is a good friend of mine who understands the paradoxical nature of accountability. Bill's easy-going and affable personality is easy to warm up to. The foundation of his personality is built upon a charitable and giving heart.

As we got to know each other, we would occasionally meet for lunch. Bill was always curious about what I was doing and how it was going. Over time our discussions turned to matters of the heart and our faith. We explored what it meant to live with impact. Bill became a voice in my life that could speak truth, question motives and challenge direction.

I would tell Bill things I had never told anyone else. Our conversations have always been private and have remained privileged. Bill models what is necessary for effective accountability. You begin engaging accountability by carefully selecting one or two people whom you trust. You are looking for a willing confidant capable of challenging and supporting you.

At the beginning of the chapter I told you about sharing a list of my top-ten most shameful and embarrassing experiences. They are private. I didn't share them, but I own them. Some had the potential to change the direction and course of my life. In the absence of growing in my knowledge, understanding and application of accountability, I am certain my race would've taken some different courses.

When Harry Truman was President of the United States, he had two signs on his desk. One quoted Mark Twain: "Always do right. This will gratify some people and astonish the rest." The other read, "The buck stops here."

> *"As iron sharpens iron, so one man sharpens another."*
> —Proverbs 27:17

You get to choose your races. Choose well. If you want to maximize your impact, never run alone—invite accountability to be your running partner.

# CHAPTER 12

# Hitting the Wall: "What it Will Take to Finish"

> "If the word quit is part of your vocabulary, then the word
> finish is likely not."
> —B. G. JETT

> "The best things in life, those of true substance, involve the
> hardest-fought battles and the longest waits."
> —JOHN HERRICK, 8 REASONS YOUR LIFE MATTERS

"Hitting the wall" was first used to describe a condition of complete physical exhaustion and mental fatigue that endurance athletes could face during their race. Picture an immovable obstacle that seemingly appears out of nowhere. It may be imaginary, but it becomes very real when it inflicts pain and suffering capable of stopping you in your tracks.

Hitting the wall is disorienting. You feel shaken and confused. Your mental vision of the finish line is wiped from view. Just taking the next step commands your full attention. You begin to think, "Hey, there is no shame in quitting—right? I gave this my best shot and that's all anyone can expect of me." Winston Churchill, standing face to face with the wall during World War II, said, "It's not enough that we do our best; sometimes we have to do what is required."

"Do your best" would seem to be more than appropriate encouragement to an 80-year-old about to run a marathon. But not if you are an

80-year-old who is attempting to complete his 29th consecutive L.A. Marathon. Stan was committed to doing what was required to finish the race. Having completed the previous 28 L.A. Marathons, Stan's goal was to maintain his exclusive standing as one of only 181 other runners to do the same.

You might quickly assume that Stan had been running his entire life—no, he had only been running half of his life. Stan assembled his impressive resume of 60 completed marathons, including the Boston Marathon, after he turned 40 years old. Proof that great goals and dreams are not a function of age.

What does an 80-year-old do to train for a marathon? Of course they cross-train on a road bike. Ten days before the race, while cross-training on his road bike, Stan pulled a hamstring muscle. Stan's doctor recommended crutches to aid his recovery. More concerning to Stan was being advised not to run the race.

When race day arrived, Stan was still in pain. His determination to run silenced all advice to the contrary. His daughter's plea to skip the race was greeted with a request to put his crutches in the car. After dropping Stan off at the starting line, family and friends gathered at mile 9 to wait for Stan and offer their encouragement and support.

Stan was well behind his normal pace when he came into view. Laboring in obvious pain as he approached the mile marker, well-wishers began offering words of consolation. There certainly would have been no shame in hitting the wall under these circumstances. "What a streak; too bad it had to come to an end." "End?" Stan thought, "who said it's coming to an end?" Stan would not hear of quitting—he was going to do what was required to finish.

Upon Stan's request, his daughter reluctantly retrieved his crutches from the car. With crutches in hand, Stan returned to the race and focused on taking the next step. At this point Stan had 100,705 feet to go to the finish line. One foot in front of the other he hobbled on. As the race timer flashed 6:35:10, Stan crossed the finish line. Good for 10th place in his age class. Stan hobbled and limped to the finish line ahead of 3,917 other runners.

The wall is an avoidable obstacle if you focus your effort and energy on doing what is required—taking the next step. You can't be reminded enough that you are an unrepeatable miracle. You alone are in a unique position to positively impact the people you love, the teams you lead and the causes that stir your heart. What will it take to finish? You've got to get your thinking right.

## Get Your Thinking Right

I love what the apostle Paul writes to the people of Corinth, "Do you not know that in a race all the runners run, but only one gets the prize? Run in such a way as to get the prize." Let that encouragement sink in—run in such a way as to get the prize! This isn't a race to do your best and be awarded a participation ribbon. You are not looking for a pat on the back—you are racing for impact, the opportunity to change lives.

"Failure is the inevitable companion of a large vision. No one can take on a significant and difficult challenge without stumbling a few times. The important thing is how we respond. The goal is not a fail-safe record, but a pattern of increasing effectiveness."[1] Failure is the inevitable companion of great goals and dreams.

> You can't expect to have impact or discover your potential without stumbling a few times along the way.

You can't expect to have impact or discover your potential without stumbling a few times along the way. The wall is out there in front of you somewhere. The wall is indiscriminate and will seemingly appear at the most inopportune times. Between you and the finish line stands a wall that will try to keep you from realizing a race rich in impact. Don't let it!

In her book *How We Can Reach Our Goals*, Dr. Heidi Grant Halvorson points out that in the course of her research she found, "No matter who they are and what they are trying to do, we find that successful people not only have confidence that they will eventually succeed, but are equally confident that they will have a tough time getting there."[2] Successful people are confident because they are filled with the unbridled hope that comes from great possibilities—hope that inspires them to take courageous action.

Henry Ford once said, "Whether you think you can or think you can't you're right."[3] Ford was right! One of the greatest challenges I ever faced was merging three businesses together that had a long history of competing with one another. *Can't* was not an option, and there was no doubt we were going to have a tough time executing the change.

## Ladies and Gentlemen, Please Welcome Mitchell

Imagine bringing three competing sales teams together and telling them we are all going to be friends now. These were competitively-driven sales people who had competed for years with one another for their livelihoods. The mere suggestion of bringing them all together for a sales meeting was akin to suggesting the Hatfields and McCoys get together for a welcoming picnic.

With the sales team's perspective shrouded in resistance and distrust, it was certainly going to be a challenge to pull together a unifying agenda for the meeting. We needed to see our situation with fresh eyes, so I invited Mitchell to speak to our team. If there was anyone who was familiar with hitting walls and figuring out what it takes to finish, it was Mitchell.

I met Mitchell a number of years ago. I had no doubt he'd have a profound impact on our team. If you had been dealt Mitchell's cards, you most likely would've quit and been excused from any expectation for delivering meaningful impact. He had plenty of people he could blame for his life's circumstances. I couldn't imagine anyone would've blamed him for proclaiming and celebrating victim status.

I asked Mitchell to close out our first day of meetings. He asked me about the mood of the room, to which I replied, "chilly." He just smiled. As I finished introducing Mitchell, he rolled out onto the stage in his wheelchair. If the wheelchair was not enough to grab everyone's attention, his disfigured hands and face could not be hidden. Mitchell made them cry, laugh and cheer as he told his story about refusing to allow two potentially life-threatening accidents to keep him from fulfilling his potential for impact.

A fiery motorcycle accident burned him beyond recognition and a plane crash took away his ability to walk. But it didn't stop him from becoming the mayor of Crested Butte, Colorado, a candidate for Congress, starting and leading a $65MM company or becoming a world-class speaker. Mitchell says, "Really, the only difference between you and me at the moment is that I had the good fortune to learn a few important points along the way—both before and after my injuries—that helped me immeasurably...I have a great life. You can have a great life, too."[4]

Our team never forgot Mitchell's transformational message. He didn't simply preach, "Pain is inevitable; suffering is optional." Mitchell lived it out. If you allow yourself to fall victim to adversity, it serves to reinforce the wall as immovable and unscalable.

The wall is resistance. It represents the challenges, frustration and pain you'll confront on your way to the finish line of any race. The wall isn't real, but it only stands tall in your mind. It wants to declare that your race is over and send you away in failure. That's what the wall is—resistance that turns pain into suffering.

Encouragement breaks the wall down, and redirects your thinking and actions towards what you can control—how to take the next step towards the finish line.

## Breaking Down The Wall

Imagine receiving a phone call from someone you are always excited to hear from. When you answer, she says, "I just called to let you know I believe in you. Don't give up on your dream. Take positive action today because you are positively impacting the people in your life. I just want to let you know I am praying for you to be filled with the energy, strength, patience and focus needed to give all you are doing your best." Then she hangs up.

You'd likely be thinking, "Wow, what just happened?" It might take you a moment to process the experience. You'd savor the feeling for a moment. Carefully replay the words in your mind. In a matter of seconds you'd realize that this unexpected phone call had breathed inspiration and optimism into your day. Your day has been changed—transformed.

Encouragement is racing fuel for the human spirit. William Arthur Ward said, "Flatter me, and I may not believe you. Criticize me, and I may not like you. Ignore me, and I may not forgive you. Encourage me and I will never forget you." We want encouragement, we need it, and we don't get enough of it. It is easy to overlook the power that encouragement has to raise confidence and inspire you to keep running in the face of resistance.

## Tapping the Power of Encouragement

Encouragement is critical to thriving and living with impact, but it is not easy to identify and align yourself with people who are encouragers. The emboldening power of an encourager is captivating because it is both powerful and rare.

The search for a true encourager is illusive. There are signs of encouragement that can draw you in only to leave you empty. We've seen examples of leaders whose words never quite match their actions, teachers who value performance over effort, coaches who sing praises in victory and assign blame in defeat, or parents whose praise always falls short of giving their blessing.

If you've taken an automobile road trip, you are familiar with "Rest Areas." They provide a quick and convenient opportunity to rest and refresh. Encouragers are the people who help you rest and refresh. These are the people you can count on when you lose heart, who pick you up in defeat, who set a great example, who never withhold their blessing in times of struggle.

Encouragers are not easy to recognize, but you can find them if you know what you are looking for. One of my most powerful memories of an encourager revealed itself during my first job upon graduating college. Just days after graduating, I started in a sales training program with Owens-Corning Fiberglas. Everything was going great until they told me I had been assigned to Los Angeles. The first thing I thought was, "How could they send me to the only place I told them I didn't want to go to?"

Do you know how big Southern California is? It can be intimidating. Any comfort I had about my destination died the night I flew into Los Angeles International Airport. Intimidating gave rise to apprehension, seeing city lights burn for nearly 25 minutes before the pilot even asked the flight attendants to prepare for arrival.

As I stood on the curb trying to figure out where to hail a cab to Long Beach, I may have even wondered aloud if I was the only person there who had no idea where they were going. My cab driver did nothing to calm my fears. He made more than a couple wrong turns and tried to drop me off more than a mile from my hotel. Eventually arriving at my hotel, I stepped out of the cab and I was looking directly at the wall.

After a restless night of sleep, I went down to breakfast the next morning to meet my new boss, Butch Ferguson. I had never met Butch, but he easily picked me out. I was the only young and seemingly nervous kid dressed like I just walked out of a Brooks Brothers sale. The moment Butch introduced himself I knew there was something special about him. Butch embodied encouragement—modeling and teaching its qualities every day.

Great encouragers keep you from hitting the wall and stir up within you the courage to finish. You need encouragement. You want encouragement. You'll get it when you are able to identify and align yourself with an encourager.

## Five Qualities Possessed by Great Encouragers

1. *A genuine heart for people*. Encouragers demonstrate a real and loving concern for people. They are keenly aware of when changing conditions and circumstances ignite fear, break hearts and rob passion.

2. *An empathetic ear.* Encouragers actively listen with empathy. They consistently seek to understand people. They are as comfortable with your fears and failures as they are with your hopes and dreams.

3. *An eye for potential.* Encouragers see people as storehouses of untapped potential. They don't see you where you are. They see where you can go and enable the discovery and development of your unique gifts and talents.

4. *A consistent source of hope.* Encouragers see circumstances and conditions as changeable. They consistently deliver words of hope that point you to the finish line.

5. *Setting a positive and inspiring example.* In every role of their life they are consistently the same. They are comfortable mixing with people from every area of their life because they are the same publicly, privately and personally.

## *Quality #1: Encouragers have a genuine heart for people.*

Real encouragement comes from the heart. "The first job of leadership is to love people," according to Rick Warren. Butch took every opportunity to expose his true heart. He, too, recently relocated to Los Angeles. Butch had a young family and a tough new assignment.

> Real encouragement comes from the heart.

Imagine entrusting your career to a bunch of rookies and misfits. The rookies were new college graduates living on their own in the big city for the first time. The misfits were new to sales or new to the company.

The one thing we shared in common was that we had no idea what we were doing. Butch should have been frustrated but instead wove us together with his heart. He genuinely cared for each of us. We became part of his family. Butch opened his home, welcomed us on holidays and stood by us in every victory and defeat. Butch had a genuine heart for people.

Encouragers recognize the potential impact and influence they have on people. They possess the rare ability to put your needs ahead of their own. Encouragers care about your mental, physical and spiritual health.

## *Quality #2: Encouragers have an empathetic ear.*

Meaningful encouragement is grounded in understanding—being able to accurately interpret what you are saying. Encouragers gain understanding by asking questions. Butch was always asking questions to gain understanding and insight. He was curious about what was happening with our jobs and lives.

Chip Ingram points out, "To be an awesome encourager, first, you need to remember that people are hurting far more than you know, and far more than they show." You need someone who willingly listens rather than quickly offering prescriptive advice or a canned response.

Butch would frequently say, "I before E—intellect before emotion," when we worked through issues or solving problems. Passion and emotion are valuable but not when making decisions. An empathetic listener patiently works through your emotion and does not let it cloud the need for understanding.

Encouragers listen with empathy. They constantly seek understanding and rely on engaging questions rather than offering advice.

### *Quality #3: Encouragers have an eye for potential.*

> Encouragers see who you are today and help equip you with the tools you will need to keep running when you hit the wall—consistently preparing you for bigger and better things that are coming your way.

Encouragers see your talent before you see it in yourself. Amazing growth and development occurs when someone helps open your eyes to fresh new possibilities. Butch constantly assessed skills, evaluated progress, observed our work and engaged us in dialogue. He helped us win in the present. More importantly, Butch prepared us for the future.

Your potential is undeniable, but you will go through periods when you will harbor doubts. An encourager always has an eye on your potential. Encouragers see who you are today and help equip you with the tools you will need to keep running when you hit the wall—consistently preparing you for bigger and better things that are coming your way.

### *Quality #4: Encouragers are a consistent source of hope.*

When you are standing at the wall in a moment of doubt or disappointment, encouragers rekindle your hope—an excitement about what's next. Hope is not positive thinking or something that is indistinguishable from wishing. Hope is a combination of your heart and your head. It is getting you to believe in a better future and encouraging you to take the action necessary to make it happen.

Prior to Butch's arrival, the L. A. division was a perennial poor performer. It had been a carousel of failed managers and sales professionals. Butch was a consistent source of hope. Andy Andrews describes how Butch used hope to break down the wall when he wrote, "Hope is the captain of courage and the author of success. For the person whose hope remains unshaken has within them the power to do miracles. Hope sees what is invisible, feels what is intangible, and achieves what most consider impossible."

Most people thought it was impossible to be successful in Los Angeles. They underestimated the power of encouragement to shape an environment of hope.

### *Quality #5: Encouragers set positive and aspiring examples.*

Albert Schweitzer won a Nobel Peace Prize in 1952 for his lifetime of medical work in Africa. Schweitzer wrote, "Example is not the main thing in influencing others. It is the only thing."[5] Great encouragers are grounded in truth that they comfortably live out in all areas of their lives. It is easy for you to look up to them and take direction from them. The example of encouragers is memorable because you see the impact they are making on the lives of the important people in their life.

Butch's example was easy to gravitate to—he loved and respected his wife, was fully committed to his role as a father, instilled confidence in the people he led and honored his commitments. He was faithful, curious, trustworthy, generous, kind, professional, patient and thoughtful. Encouragers set positive and inspiring examples.

## Who Encourages You?

Aligned with sources of encouragement, you will find your way to the starting line more easily and find the motivation to accelerate races that have stalled. Edmund Lee, a prominent legal and political figure in Colonial America, said, "Surround yourself with the dreamers and the doers, the believers and thinkers, but most of all, surround yourself with those who see the greatness within you, even when you don't see it yourself." The wall is out there, but encouragement will help you avoid hitting it on your way to the finish line.

Who encourages you? Who are you surrounding yourself with on a regularly basis. These are the people who are going to largely determine the speed and quality of your race. During a coaching conversation with a young man who has tremendous talent and ambition, I asked him, "Where do you want to be five years from now?" He quickly and easily began to paint a future reflecting lofty ambition.

I then asked him to tell me about the people he spends the most time with away from work. Interestingly he started by telling me a story about his weekend. He described a great group of friends who he enjoys spending time with but who do not share his ambition. He went on to express frustration about how he frequently is the shepherd of his friends.

You know the next question. "Who are your sources of encouragement," I asked? He thought about it for a moment and said, "I may need to get some new friends." What about you? Think for a moment about the five people you spend the most time with. Now ask yourself, "How much encouragement do I receive from each of them?" Consider the qualities of an encourager. For each of the five people you identified, categorize their encouragement factor as positive, neutral or negative. If the sum of your evaluation is leaning towards the negative, take note. You, too, may need some new friends.

Identifying and nurturing relationships with encouragers is critical to developing the resources and tools you will need to avoid hitting the walls that stand between you and the finish line.

## What It Will Take to Finish!

The wall is out there, built brick by brick. Each brick handpicked and layered on the wall by experience—adversity, disappointment, doubt, discouragement, regret and fear. The wall eventually rises up to meet all of us. How you finish, the quality of your impact, will be determined by what you do when the wall appears.

St. Paul's Cathedral is one of the most famous cultural and architectural landmarks in London. The celebrated architect Christopher Wren was commissioned as its designer. Wren is said to have been walking through the building site, asking the workers what they were doing. One man told him he was doing carpentry work, another was laying bricks, yet another explained he was putting the stained glass into place, and a fourth man pointed out he was carving stone. As Wren was leaving the construction site, he came upon a man mixing mortar and again asked the question, "What are you doing?" Not aware who Wren was, he proudly replied, "Sir, I am a mason and I am building a great cathedral."[6]

Randy Pausch was a professor of computer science and human-computer interaction and design at Carnegie Mellon University. Pausch went from an obscure professor to a thought leader on running strong and finishing with impact when his book, The Last Lecture, was published. Pausch's book was his response to a terminal cancer diagnosis with only a few months to live. Pausch says, "The brick walls are there for a reason. The brick walls are not there to keep us out. The brick walls are there to give us a chance to show how badly we want something. Because the brick walls are there to stop the people who don't want it badly enough."[7]

## *Tough enough to finish*

Pausch is describing toughness that isn't physical. It is not about strength or physical ability. Pausch is talking about a toughness that helped him finish strong. The same toughness that propelled Stan to finish his 29th L.A. Marathon and allowed Mitchell to overcome two life-threatening accidents. A toughness that rises with encouragement, brought to life within us by encouragers.

Every race you run will present you with a unique set of conditions, circumstances and preparedness. Finishers share one thing in common—great thinking supported by mental toughness. Mike Krzyzewski, the winningest coach in college basketball history, said, "The end is when you most often meet the forces that can stop you from completing the effort. You don't let those forces in, and you don't make it monumental. Completion is just the next step in the process."[8]

Consider Sage Steele's rise to prominence as a sports anchor for ESPN. Steele's father was the first African-American to play varsity football at West Point in 1966. He made Sage memorize the Cadet Prayer of the United States Military Academy. In part it reads,

"Encourage us in our endeavor to live above the common level of life. Make us to choose the harder right instead of the easier wrong, and never to be content with a half-truth when the whole can be won. Endow us with courage that is born of loyalty to all that is noble and worthy, that scorns to compromise with vice and injustice and knows no fear when truth and right are in jeopardy."[9]

Steele climbed a tough road to reach her goal to become an ESPN anchor. The motto instilled a foundation of great thinking—tough thinking. The thinking it will take to finish. You are going to come upon walls. It doesn't matter how they got there...expect them. Remember they are not there to stop you...only to challenge your commitment to finish the race.

What will it take to finish? Surround yourself with encouragement that builds toughness to support you every step of the way.

# CHAPTER 13

# Hazards: "Warning Signs, Detours, and Second Chances"

*"Fear may fill our world, but it doesn't have to fill our hearts."*
—MAX LUCADO, AUTHOR, *FEARLESS*

*"Life begins at the edge of your comfort zone."*
—ED GARRISON

They were everywhere. How did we miss them—prominent, visible and plentiful. "No Shoulder," "Falling Rock" and "Narrow Winding Road Next 8 Miles." They are common road signs you regularly see along the side of roads. But this time they would take on new meaning.

I focused my full attention on the road while my wife sat back and enjoyed the incredible scenery. Enjoyment turned to tension as the road narrowed and started to switch back and forth through a series of hairpin turns. Tension grew in my arms and hands as I gripped the steering wheel tighter. Every few hundred feet felt like a mile as we crept along. We kept thinking the worst was behind us, but the road—really no more than a path—just kept getting more demanding.

At one point we were inching up a hill in our rental car flanked by a nearly vertical rock wall on our right and a cavernous cliff on our left. The only guardrail was the overgrown trees that scraped against the side of the car. At the crest of the hill stood a man anxiously waving us up. He was urging us to hurry as he held back traffic from going down this "highway" barely wide enough for our car.

We didn't plan on making this "white-knuckle" drive on the Kahekili Highway. Our plan was to enjoy the beautiful Maui scenery on a leisurely drive back to Wailea from Kapalua. Later, a little research revealed the real meaning of the warning signs, "Once you are in, it is almost impossible to change your minds and head back, as there is simply no space to do so."[1] "It is a legendary road known for its snaking turns, narrow passages, and dangerous road conditions...this dangerous road needles around hairpin turns, careens over one-lane bridges and teeters beside treacherous cliffs. It's one of Maui's most adventurous drives... perhaps it's for the thrill of driving on the edge of a cliff."[2]

I was not interested in driving on the edge of a cliff. Is anyone? If I read the rental car agreement, I'd have known that driving a rental car on the Kahekili Highway is strictly prohibited. But who reads rental car agreements—right?

## A Warning About Life

If something had happened to our rental car, can you hear their first words? Exactly. "Didn't you read the agreement?" We all know the answer to that question. "Of course I didn't read the agreement; who reads the fine print?" So, what would you do if someone handed you a racing agreement for your life, spelling out all of the risks and prohibited activities? Exactly. You'd tuck it away for future reference.

For future reference, here are two warnings you would find in the fine print. The first warning: "You may not follow all of the elements of this agreement. When you screw up, be prepared to hear 'I told you so.'" You know there is always someone ready to pounce on your mistakes and let you know it. The second warning: "There are no guarantees in life, except death and taxes." In other words, proceed at your own risk.

Benjamin Franklin was certainly correct about death and taxes. He should have added—your race will not turn out like you plan. There is an often-quoted axiom: "The best-laid plans of mice and men oft go astray."[3] This translates to the modern axiom: "You can be guaranteed your race will not turn out exactly as you planned."

> "You can be guaranteed your race will not turn out exactly as you planned."

Quietly and unexpectedly your race can be hijacked by the seemingly endless stream of life's temporary inconveniences. A slow progression of converting uninvited irritations from momentary distractions into reasons for failed plans and incomplete races. My grandmother raised 12 kids and celebrated 48 grandchildren. She faced constant waves of temporary inconveniences. She would say, "There is no reason to cry over spilled milk—clean it up and pour another glass." She possessed an immovable spirit. My grandmother just would not allow life's temporary inconveniences to take her off course.

Heartbreak does not clean up like spilled milk. When you run into family, relational, career, financial or health issues, they can deliver a blow so profound it will take every ounce of strength and resilience you have to get back in the race. History and experience show us that no one gets to the finish line without navigating stretches of road filled with snaking turns, narrow passages and dangerous conditions that leave you feeling like you are teetering on the edge of a treacherous cliff.

There will be warning signs over the course of your race, but they won't stop you from finding yourself on the Kahekili Highway with one option—finish the race!

## Personal Inflection Points

Life's warning signs are crafted from your experience and knowledge. They are hints of wisdom and instinct that ping your brain like an alert on your phone, pointing out both impending danger and potential opportunity. They'll beg you to slow down and evaluate your situation, as well as urge you to take action.

Looking back, it is easy to identify the warning signs. They are checkered throughout our race path as personal inflection points (PIPs). PIPs are events or experiences you encounter during your race that command your attention and profoundly impact or change the course of your race.

"We experience approximately 20,000 individual moments a day according to Nobel Prize-winning scientist Daniel Kahneman. Each moment lasts but a few seconds and rarely do we recall a neutral encounter. The memorable moments are either positive or negative. Kahneman's research showed that a single encounter can change your life forever."[4] Encounters that define your life's personal inflection points. PIPs serve as catalysts to propel you towards the finish line or blow up the road in front of you—sidelining you or sending you on a detour.

## *You Gotta Keep Dancin!*

Tim Hansel was the founder of Summit Expedition—a wilderness survival school. In his book *You Gotta Keep Dancin'*, Tim describes the power and influence of personal inflection points. A survival expert with extensive hiking and climbing experience, Tim is familiar with danger, risk and warning signs.

In 1975 Tim and two friends embarked on a hike into the Sierra Mountains. They had a simple goal—lunch with a view. Not just any view but a view from 14,000 feet. Tim acknowledges the danger and warning signs of what is in front of them when he writes, "Moving with deliberateness, but not hurry. Hurry forgets, makes mistakes. In situations like this, mistakes can be fatal...we check our equipment twice...the trick is to find the perfect balance between lightness and completeness...too much weight is dangerous...likewise too little equipment is dangerous."

Tim described the top of the mountain as "a view worth the time, risk, and effort." On their descent they had to cross back over a snow bridge that they knew would be changing its complexion over the course of the day because "snow has many personalities." Tim describes the scene: "We can see the tent in the distance. We feel secure in crampons, standing eight to ten feet above crevasse. At that angle it is no more difficult than standing on a roof."

Tim's partner David was half way across the bridge when Tim's crampons filled up with ice, and he began to fall. Unable to arrest his fall he landed upside down on the ice below. Tim was shaken, stunned and unaware of what had just happened to his body. Tim's hike down the mountain with the aid of his partners is nothing short of a miracle in light of what he would discover over the coming days and months.

The fall inflicted permanent damage on Tim's body—multiple fractures of the vertebrae, crushed discs, bone fragments in the neck that resulted in a state of intense permanent pain, fatigue and traumatic deteriorating arthritis.[5]

Tim describes his personal inflection point this way: "This journey which I believe is sacred, almost cost me my life and my family. One night I was speaking about the genuine, concrete, tangible, inextinguishable joy I've discovered in the process and a man came up to me afterwards and said, 'You almost make me want to fall into a crevasse so I can discover how special life really is.'"[6]

I've read and referred to Tim's book many times. It sits prominently on a bookshelf close to my desk to remind me that the race for impact is filled with warning signs, hazards, and detours. Personal inflection points will define your race. The key is that you must write the definition. Hansel says, "Each of us gets a second chance every day. If we would just open our eyes to the possibilities...My life, my story, turned out differently from my original script."

## Don't Let Anything Rob You of Your Passion

Warnings signs aren't there to stop you but to command your attention and prepare you for what lies ahead. Your roles can change in an unexpected moment, but it does not change your potential or responsibility to finish the race.

I joke that if life turned out the way I planned, I'd have a lot more hair—even a little hair would be good. Simple realities in our lives constantly remind us that we will face hazards on our way to the finish line. You can know it and accept it, but it doesn't stop the hazards from trying to rob you of your passion. You can even know a personal inflection point is on the horizon, but you won't understand or feel its magnitude until it actually happens.

I was quickly approaching a personal inflection point in 2001. Cancer does that. No one plans for cancer—it sneaks up on you without warning. Cancer doesn't ask for permission to interrupt your race. I had no idea how it was going to change my race or even that I would allow it to interrupt my race—it wasn't my cancer.

But if you have any experience with cancer, you know it has a long reach. The reach in this case is summed up in the context of family. John was my wife's cousin's husband. A bit convoluted but stick with me for a moment. My wife and her cousin Kathleen are very close. They are nearly the same age, grew up just blocks apart and attended the same schools—close. As their lives unfolded they continued to share the same experiences—marriage, relocating to Southern California, children and again living nearby each other. Shared experiences bring people together and love binds you together.

Our families were close. Our kids are the best of friends. John was a loving and devoted husband and father. It shook the core of our family when John was diagnosed with throat cancer. Before he lost his fight with cancer in 2003, he asked me to help and support Kathleen, Johnny (12), Nicholas (11) and Katherine (5). I hadn't even remotely thought about what it would be like to have two families.

Just like Tim Hansel, my plans changed. On the new course, a few doors closed—my career progression and destination were changed forever. A few doors opened—the joy of lasting and significant impact grew beyond measure. Personal inflection points expose quickly who we are. They easily and clearly identify who we love and what we are willing to do to run with impact. Speaking at John's funeral, I said, "All of our lives are terminal; only time and quality differ."

> Without passion, life's hazards become the story of your race rather than the impact that resulted from your race.

You can't know the length of your time, but you can passionately pursue impact each and every day. You can't let anything rob you of your passion. Passion brings energy to everything you do. Without passion, life's hazards become the story of your race rather than the impact that resulted from your race. As Nelson Mandela said, "There is no passion to be found playing small—in settling for a life that is less than the one you are capable of living."

## Five Signs You Are Losing Your Passion

Without passion your race is over. Your passion must be guarded and cherished because it is the fuel that will carry you to the finish line. Passion is a strong and barely controllable emotion that is sustaining, energizing and differentiating. Passion is neither elusive nor unrecognizable, but it is always under attack. Passion keeps you from throwing in the towel or admitting defeat.

You know what passion can do. You have seen, felt and experienced what happens when you are passionate about your roles, goals and dreams—moments when you felt the impact from your efforts. Pause for a moment and think of a time in your life when you were truly passionate. How easy was it to get excited about what you were doing? How much joy did you feel about the impact you were creating? The fuel to finish is passion.

Guard against anything robbing you of your passion by learning to recognize four warning signs. Undiagnosed or left unaddressed, they will affect your stamina and ability to run with strength and courage.

## Warning Sign #1: Fatigue

Vince Lombardi, the great coach of the Green Bay Packers, encouraged his players to push through physical weariness by reminding them, "Fatigue makes cowards of us all."[7] Lombardi's goal was for his players to be in superior physical condition in order to combat the effects of fatigue.

How do you perform when you are tired? How does anyone perform when they are tired? Performance suffers! The medical definition of fatigue is a state of physical and/or mental exhaustion that can be triggered by stress, medication, overwork, or mental and physical illness or disease.[8] Lombardi was right about fatigue giving rise to cowardice because no one has an endless supply of energy.

Researchers consistently conclude that fatigue adversely impacts performance because the body is weakened, response time is slowed, mental focus is lost and intellectual agility blurred. Every day your physical, intellectual and emotional activities burn energy. Your energy tank is replenished based on your habits around sleep, diet and exercise. But once you start running on empty, fatigue sets in.

A lack of balance in your life is a warning sign for fatigue. Every year in my business we conducted an organizational talent assessment. We used 64 different competencies to profile every individual's strengths and weaknesses. One of the 64 competencies was "Work/Life Balance." We had some leaders who believed that this competency should never appear on a profile. They would declare, "It is not relevant to talent evaluation or potential." They would go as far as questioning why anyone would need to work on improving this competency.

I don't know anyone who doesn't struggle with the idea of maintaining life balance. Balance, by definition, suggests the potential to fall and suffer harm. The very nature of balance can be stressful because it is not only difficult to achieve, it is difficult to maintain.

It may be more valuable to think in terms of blending your races. We all know there are going to be times where a race is going to command a disproportionate amount of your time, attention and focus. Let me use marriage as an example. Marriage is not a 50/50 proposition—no healthy relationship is. It will ebb and flow, requiring more or less of you depending on the changing requirements of your other roles and responsibilities.

The relationship cannot remain unbalanced in either direction indefinitely or it will fail. Every important role priority can never be perfectly balanced, but it can be appropriately blended to accommodate changing circumstances and requirements.

You need balance or blending, and you also need sleep to combat fatigue. "Like a drunk," Harvard sleep expert Charles A. Czeisler wrote, "a person who is sleep deprived has no idea how functionally impaired he or she truly is. Most of us have forgotten what it really feels like to be awake."[10]

Could more sleep be better? Tony Schwartz, President of The Energy Project, wrote, "Too many of us continue to live by the durable myth that one less hour of sleep gives us one more hour of productivity. In reality, each hour less of sleep not only leaves us feeling more fatigued, but also takes a pernicious toll on our cognitive capacity. The more consecutive hours we are awake and the fewer we sleep at night, the less alert, focused and efficient we become, and the lower the quality of our work."[11]

It looks like Lombardi was right when he said that "fatigue does make cowards of us all." Take positive steps every day to build up your energy so you will have the strength and courage to run with impact. Schwartz's advice—"Gonna thrive while I'm alive, I'll sleep so I'm ahead."

## Warning Sign #2: Frustration

Frustration is the emotion that starts bubbling up when effort and expectation do not match up with results. Our natural response to unfinished work and disappointing progress is frustration. It can be as simple as being late for a meeting due to traffic and as complicated as a failing relationship. The frustration response is not something we need to be taught; it is part of our emotional makeup.

I remember a toy my boys played with when they were very young. It was called a "shapes sorter cube." You've seen them, maybe played with one. Picture a hollow cube with holes carved in the sides representing various shapes—circle, square, star and triangle. There was a three-dimensional molded piece to match each of these shapes. The object of the game was to slip each of the unique pieces into the matching shape on the cube.

Joy would turn to frustration when they could not get a piece to fit. Natural competitiveness would spur them to keep trying. But unrewarded effort eventually turns to anger. You know how this story ends. Their anger eventually turns to apathy and they lose interest in the game. Without interest, what reason is there to continue? It's time to quit.

The unimpeded cycle of frustration, anger and apathy kills passion and crushes performance. When you are in the development phase of a new race—learning something new, doing something different or working in a new environment—you must recognize that frustration is a part of the race. It is like being handed a complicated "shapes sorter cube" and having to figure out how to make it all go together. Recognition is the first step to arrest frustration from robbing you of your passion.

Frustration is a powerful force and can take you off course very quickly. Few things can be as frustrating as travel problems. On one particular flight home, through Atlanta, I sat on the plane waiting for a gate to open so I could make a connecting flight. It was going to be "Just a few minutes," the pilot announced before we could get into the gate. A few is three or so, right? Not in airline time! After many more than a few minutes passed with no movement, passengers grew impatient and began openly expressing their frustration.

After sitting for 45 minutes, frustration had simmered to a boil. Angry passengers were pressing for information about their connecting flights. When the plane finally began to advance towards the gate the pilot tried to bring calm to the pending mad dash for the exit. He began by thanking everyone for their patience which was met with a chorus of "What about our connections!" The pilot then assured us that our connecting flight teams were waiting for us, which was met with groans of disbelief.

With a glimmer of hope, I arrived at my connecting gate just in time to see the last flight to Orange County pushing away from the jetway. The prospect of staying overnight in Atlanta was not appealing, so I got in line to inquire about getting a seat on the last flight to Los Angeles. By the time I got to the counter the gate agent had been deflecting a steady ambush of angry travelers.

Passenger after passenger turned away from the gate agent after angrily pleading their case. I learned by watching what was taking place that misplaced frustration and anger was not the winning strategy. When I stepped to the counter I said, "Tough day! Can I get you a cup of coffee?" She began shaking her head and shot me a disbelieving look. Then she asked me for my boarding pass. As I handed it to her she said, "Black, please."

Asking for my boarding pass while she shook her head confused me. Nonetheless I promptly located a Starbucks. I quickly returned and handed her a large cup of hot black coffee. She shook her head again and handed me back what I thought was my old boarding pass. I looked more closely and began to smile. Nearly simultaneously we said, "Thank you." She had a fresh cup of coffee. I was in a first-class seat on the last flight to L. A.

Frustration drains passion and kills ambition. It is an early warning system alerting you to intercede and circumvent its advance. The warning of frustration will not lay dormant if unaddressed. It begs a response. It says, "What you are currently doing is not working. Now what are you going to do?" You can let it frame up a weak excuse to justify delaying or ending your race or push you to look for the next best step and take it.

## Warning Sign #3: Failure

Few things are as painful as pouring your heart into something only to fall short of the finish line. Failure doesn't plan on just coming for a visit. It will gladly take up residence in your heart and mind. It thrives on your sense of loss and uses the emotional defeat to raise up barriers to deflect pain. Who hasn't failed and said, "I am never going to do that again."

Running healthy, meaningful and impactful races will not be devoid of failure. Zig Ziglar, the great motivational speaker, said, "Failure is a detour, not a dead-end street." Failure is normal, but do you know anyone who likes to fail? When you reach a point where the prospect of failure stands in the way of you and the finish line, it is a warning sign. You can't let failure take up residence and keep you from finishing races you were called to run.

> "Failure is a detour, not a dead-end street."
> —Zig Ziglar

Failure can drain even the most committed runners of their passion. Og Mandino, the best-selling author of *The Greatest Secret*, said, "Failure will never overtake me if my determination to succeed is strong enough." Determination is not just drawing upon random motivational and inspirational musings. Fierce and inspired determination rises and falls in direct proportion to your *why*.

*Why* defines the impact you want to deliver. *Why* leaves no doubt about your commitment to developing and using your unique talent regardless of the prospect of failure. *Why* is your answer to these questions.

- Who will benefit?
- How will they benefit?
- What do I get?
- What will this mean?
- Why does it matter?

When you understand why you are doing something, you don't allow failure to become the excuse for not remaining committed to your critical roles. Your focus on the finish line is razor sharp and you embrace how each of your races creates your greatest opportunities for delivering meaningful impact.

Failure should have consumed Abraham Lincoln. Heading into the 1860 presidential election, Abraham Lincoln was a failure, by nearly all accounts. Lincoln grew up in poverty, lost eight elections, twice failed in business, and suffered a nervous breakdown. In the years leading up to his run for the presidency, he lost a bid for the U. S. Senate in 1854, received less than 100 votes in his attempt to secure the Vice Presidential nomination in 1856, and then failed again in running for a Senate seat in 1858.

But Lincoln became arguably the best president in the history of the United States. In the aggregate rankings from 18 surveys of presidential achievements, leadership qualities, failures and faults, from 1948 to 2015, Abraham Lincoln was in the top three in all 18 surveys—he topped the rankings in ten of the surveys.[12]

Abraham Lincoln stood before Congress in December 1862. "He closed his speech with the following eloquent passage: 'We know how to save the Union. In giving freedom to the slave, we assure freedom to the free—honorable alike in what we give, and what we preserve. We shall nobly save, or meanly lose, the last best hope of earth.'"[13]

Commanding clarity of why you are running is richly deterministic, willingly acknowledging failure but not yielding to it. Abraham Lincoln's *why* was "his vision of America as a land of opportunity and a government based on democratic ideals."[14] Lincoln acknowledged his failings, but his passion was fueled with undaunted determination to run with impact and finish strong.

As B. F. Skinner, the influential behavioral psychologist said, "A failure is not always a mistake, it may simply be the best one can do under the circumstances. The real mistake is to stop trying."

## Warning Sign #4: Fear

The fear I experienced driving the Kahekili Highway was real. You probably have a similar memory of clear and present danger. We've all experienced it. Your body prepares to fight or flee. Researchers call it the "acute stress response."[15] Fear triggers real chemical changes in your body—your heart rate increases, breathing accelerates, blood rushes to your brain and muscles, your palms sweat, muscles contract and pupils dilate.

The perception of fear is equally real. I remember a time when my wife woke me to tell me she thought someone had broken into our house—she was so frightened she was shaking uncontrollably. I got up and checked every door and window of the house. I returned, assuring her she was safe. But her perceived fear left her trembling for hours.

Your possibility box full of dreams, goals and ambition is squeezed by fear. However strong your desire is to finish your race it can be subdued and potentially overwhelmed by fear.

The job that provided the springboard for my career was a 100%-commissioned sales position—I only got paid when I sold something. On top of that I was responsible for all of my own expenses—making the job even riskier. Entering the growth phase of this critical race, I was a newlywed with a new mortgage. With very little money in the bank, I was feeling the pressure. Failure was not an option. I had to close sales every day. On the outside I was projecting opportunity but on the inside I was oozing fear.

Within a few months I was diagnosed with Crohn's disease. I'll spare you the details of how it manifested itself and give you the Mayo Clinic's medical definition—"An inflammation of the lining of the digestive tract...Crohn's disease can be both painful and debilitating, and may lead to life-threatening complications...there is no known cure."[16]

After a full array of exams, lab tests and diagnostics, the doctor was certain of the diagnosis. They were also convinced that the source of my condition was stress. Fear was simply manifesting itself in my body in a frightening way. Fear is a powerful warning sign that can take you off course quickly—potentially sidelining your race.

Fear tries to push you to safety, establishing false boundaries well inside of your amazing potential. Fear squeezes the dreams, goals and ambition out of your possibility box. What remains is not what you could do but what you are willing to do. Fear is the small voice in your head that says you can't do it, it won't work, you'll fail, no one will buy it, you can't sell it, you can't win, no one will read it, they won't acknowledge you, or add your favorite reason to the list.

> **Fear tries to push you to safety, establishing false boundaries well inside of your amazing potential.**

Fear is where your confidence butts up against perceived risk. This raw sense of danger and risk is a constant and relentless force whose objective is to drain the vital passion you need to run and finish the important races in your life. David Schwartz, best selling author of *The Magic of Thinking*

*Big*, wrote, "Do what you fear and fear disappears."[17] Fear is a warning sign that begs you to push back.

When my oldest son, Matthew, was three, he refused to take some medicine. I attempted to break through his fear of taking the medicine by getting him to agree that it would be "not that bad." To suppress his momentary fear in exchange for feeling better, he agreed that taking the medicine would be, "not that bad."

I sat Matthew up on the counter and asked, "What do you think?" He replied, "Not that bad." "Perfect," I thought. I measured the medication into the dropper. Then I inserted it in his mouth and squeezed. He held the medication in his smiling cherub cheeks as I encouraged him to swallow it. I gave him a big encouraging smile and said, "Remember, it's not that bad." He looked me right in the eye and spit it out all over me. The corners of his mouth rose into a big smile. Then he proudly announced, "Not that bad."

As you would expect Matthew, eventually learned to push his fears aside. Yes, he took his medicine and got better. Fear is an ever-present race companion presenting unwelcome resistance. As a young man working his way through college, law school and the bar exam, Matthew faced plenty of fears and resistance. When his fear presented no clear and present danger, all I had to say was, "not that bad," and he understood he had a choice to make. His fear was warning him not to give in but push back by taking decisive action.

You get stronger and gain confidence when you lean into a fear because after you do the very thing you feared, you eventually figure out it is "not that bad."

## Warning Sign #5: Fun

At first glance, you might not expect to see *fun* on a warning sign. But the lack of fun may be the most important warning sign. It is so easy to get fixated on the finish line. With eyes set straight ahead and all attention focused on getting to the end of the race, you fail to enjoy the experience of the journey.

Who hasn't felt stressed and weighed down by deadlines and expectations? Think of a time where you crossed the finish line of an important race and felt little satisfaction or joy. You may have even said aloud, "Is this it? Is this what a sought-after achievement is supposed to feel like?"

When I observed that people were stressed and pressing, I liked to ask, "Where are you on the fun meter?" The first time someone heard this they would most likely flash back a confused look. "Go ahead," I would press, "on a scale of 1 to 10, how much fun are you having?" The warning is simple. If you consistently find yourself on the low end of the *fun meter*, it is a warning sign.

The truth about fun and the laughter that comes with it is that when you're willing to lighten up, nothing will be so important or serious that it robs you of your passion and blinds you to the many blessings and opportunities in your life. Consider the fact that laughter has helped cure cancer, relieved pain, been the foundation of successful careers, healed relationships, held teams and families together and is valued and embraced in many great companies and organizations.

Have you ever seen anyone dying from laughter?—neither have I. But it is not a stretch to see people suffering and dying because they are not laughing and having fun. The laughter that comes from having fun is an inexhaustible resource that is an essential ingredient for generating impact and finishing the important races in your life. Laughing activates 80 muscles that lead to greater health and well-being. No wonder Mark Twain said, "Against the assault of laughter, nothing can stand."

## It Will All Make Sense

Nothing of lasting and meaningful impact was ever accomplished without passion. Your journey will be filled with hazards—those personal inflection points that grab your attention and profoundly impact or change your life. Pay attention to the warning signs, accept the detours and maximize your second chances.

There will be days when you can't see the finish line—just take the next step.

There will be days when you question taking the next step—revitalize your *why*.

There will be days when your *why* doesn't seem to be enough—pray for wisdom.

There will be days when you are taking yourself way too seriously—lighten up and find a reason to laugh.

There will be days when you don't understand the blessings and tragedies of life, and why things aren't going like you planned—give thanks to God.

There will be a day when you enter the stadium and see why you kept running and striving for impact—then it will make sense.

# CHAPTER 14

## Getting Back on Track: "So Many Races, So Little Time"

*"If you do not change direction, you may end up where you are heading."*
—*LAO TZU*

Have you ever been lost but didn't want to turn around or change direction? Few things are worse than making good time and being told you are going the wrong way. Every man knows this. Every woman has observed it. A man behind the wheel of a car is never lost. Well, at least not until he admits he is really lost.

My directions showed it was only 20 minutes from our hotel. My sons and I loaded up and were making very good time. We anticipated arriving early for the Spring training baseball game between the Texas Rangers and the Kansas City Royals. Our plan was to leave plenty of time to collect autographs and check out the Rangers' brand new training facility in Surprise, Arizona.

After 20 minutes of driving, all we could see was desert. Could I possibly be lost? The boys suggested I call Mom. I could think of few things worse than calling my wife and asking for directions, but we were running out of time. "Hey, just called to see how you are doing," I say. "By the way, can you check some directions for me?" Now laughing, she replies, "You're lost." We were more than lost. We were driving in the wrong direction. Have you ever been lost but didn't want to admit to it?

It was hard to admit we were lost, but it was the key to getting back on track. C. S. Lewis was right when he said, "We all want progress, but if you're on the wrong road, progress means doing an about-turn and walking back to the right road; in that case, the man who turns back soonest is the most progressive."

## Choose to Be Progressive

The question is not whether you are going to get lost—you will. Everyone does. We hate admitting we are lost because it screams failure. Few things weigh on us more than failure. We all know we wouldn't care about failing if the race didn't matter, but it does. Dr. Jeffery Brown, in his book *The Competitive Edge*, explores the nature of successfully competing. Dr. Brown points out, "A good litmus test for whether a competition is legitimate is to determine whether your performance could have ended in failure. Remember, if you can't possibly fail, then you're probably not competing."[1]

Your race for impact is the pinnacle of competition. Take solace in the fact that if you feel lost you are competing. Lost is losing sight of an important role and suffering a performance setback. Lost is failing to maintain your investment in a critical role and scrambling to rebuild a relationship and make up for lost time. Lost is suffering a significant personal loss. Lost is facing a challenging professional crossroad. Lost is valuing possessions over relationships and experiences. Lost is discovering that there is nothing you can buy to fill your desire for impact. Lost is struggling to act on the dreams stirring in your soul.

Even the best races will have their share of brokenness and interruption. Getting lost and failing are part of the race journey. Make no mistake about it...you are engaged in a legitimate competition where failure means disappointing the people you care about most. Taking the competition seriously means fighting every day to align your effort and focus on the roles and goals that provide the greatest opportunity for you to create impact.

Dr. Laura Nash and her colleague Dr. Howard Stevenson have concluded that we have a deep yearning for impact. Authors of *Just Enough*, Dr. Nash and Dr. Stevenson were curious to discover what drives people who have led impactful lives. They conducted comprehensive research, reviewed case studies, conducted interviews with high achievers, and did extensive tests of their model in search of understanding our most significant motivations. They concluded, "There are four components to success that people seek in their lives—achievement, happiness, significance and legacy."[2]

These are the fruits of an impactful race. When the impact you are delivering, in your most important roles, falls short of your vision for achievement, happiness, significance and legacy, you are going to find yourself on the wrong road. This is the time, as Lewis suggested, to be progressive and get back on track.

## On Your Mark, Get Set, Go!

When you hear the words just do it, what do you think of? Good chance you said, "Nike." The phrase is a trademarked element of the iconic Nike brand. "Just Do It" has become a part of our pop culture—a call to action.

Action expends energy and creates movement, but it does not guarantee that you are on the right path. Every year thousands of experienced hikers get lost. The very nature of being lost sparks fear and confusion. Hikers who have gotten lost describe being overcome with a sense of loneliness. The disorientation of being lost is overwhelming and can cause panic. A bad situation becomes worse because bad decisions lead to wasting precious energy and resources.[2]

"Just Do It" makes for great commercials, but it can make a bad situation worse if you are lost. Getting back on track requires a plan. Joel Barker, a leading futurist said, "Vision without action is merely a dream. Action without vision just passes the time. Vision with action can change the world...it is in the future where our greatest leverage is. We can't change the past, although we can learn from it. Things happen in only one place—the present. And usually we react to those events...It is the yet-to-be, the future, and only there, where we have the time to prepare for the present."[3]

Vision brought to life with action is the key to running races that create lasting and meaningful impact. Getting back on track can be challenging but does not require an elaborate or laborious process. You can refocus and re-energize your race by employing three steps that draw upon the principles we have already explored.

1. On your mark: Clarify your roles and goals.
2. Get set: Connect to your source of power.
3. Go: Commit to build a plan and take action.

# On Your Mark

### *Where did you say you were going?*

Clarity is imagining the future today. It's the picture of the race you want to run described from the finish line looking backwards. Clarity defines the path to the finish line, including who you are going to touch and what you are going to achieve while running the race. The mission of your race is to convert your vision into reality. Where did you say you were going?

Getting lost on the way to the finish line occurs for one of two reasons. Either you haven't taken time to paint a picture of your race to the finish line or your vision has become fuzzy. Your vision of the finish line is how you define the quality of your life (achievement and happiness), increasing your capacity for service (significance) and maximizing your impact (legacy).

### *Painting your picture?*

Energy and excitement are reignited when you have a clear and vivid picture of your finish line. When Jim Carrey was a struggling actor, he painted a picture. Carrey wrote himself a check for $10 million in 1990. He post-dated the check 1994. On the memo line he wrote "for acting service rendered." Carrey put the check in his wallet and looked at it every day. For his 1994 role in *Dumb and Dumber*, Jim Carrey was paid exactly $10 million.[5]

In a 2014 commencement address Carrey said, "I learned many, many lessons from my father, but not least of which is that you can fail at something you don't want, so you might as well take a chance doing what you love."[6]

What does your finish line picture look like? Imagine breaking the tape at the finish line. You take a deep breath and begin looking around the stadium. Feel the exhilaration of the cheering and applause—the thrill of victory. The stands are filled with an appreciative crowd of people whose lives were enriched and rewarded by how you ran your race.

There are two distinct and powerful benefits you accrue from clarifying your role focus and commitment. First, it defines who you need to be in order to touch the hearts and minds of the people you want to be remembered by. Second, it commands your attention to focus on what you want to be remembered for.

Vivid clarity is vital to generating the longevity and persistence you will need to finish your races strong. Fred Rogers is best known as the star and host of the award-winning television show Mr. Rogers Neighborhood. Fred Rogers created lasting and sustaining impact by developing a crystal-clear vision of his most important roles. Role clarity and commitment inspired and motivated Mr. Rogers to produce 895 original episodes of the longest-running show in PBS history.[7]

Fred Rogers was committed to helping kids discover their unique worth. His passion was helping kids explore their potential for running great races. In 1997 Fred Rogers received a Lifetime Achievement Award from the National Academy of Television Arts and Sciences. Fred Rogers' acceptance speech describes the victory that comes from the pursuit of a clear vision.

"So many people have helped me to come to this night...All of us have special ones who have loved us into being. Would you just take 10 seconds to think of the people who have helped you become who you are? Those who have helped you become who you are, those who have cared about you, and wanted what was best for you in life...Whomever you've been thinking about—how pleased they must be to know the difference you feel they've made. Thank you...for encouraging me, allowing me to be your neighbor."[8]

Clarity kept Fred Rogers on the path to the finish line he envisioned. Clarity will do the same for you. Who is in your picture? You'll get back on track and stay on track by committing your time, talent and resources to excellence in the roles that impact the people you love, the teams you lead and the causes that stir your heart.


## Life comes at you fast

So many races...so little time! An alarm goes off for most people when they stand on the finish line and see all the opportunities for impact and realize their most scarce resource is time. You might say, "Life comes at you fast." TM Advertising created a very successful ad campaign for Nationwide Insurance entitled "Life Comes at You Fast." Describing the campaign, TM Advertising said, "We decided to take a dramatic approach—blending subtle humor and stark reality to emphasize how quickly life passes you by."[9]

My favorite ad begins with a man standing in his garage looking at two switches on the wall. The door from the garage to the kitchen is open. You can see his wife sitting at a table working. As he reaches for the switches, he says, "Honey, do you know what this light switch does?" "Which one?" she asks. "The one on the right," he replies. "I don't know. I never use that one," she says. He begins to flip the switch up and down while asking her to look and see if it turns anything on. "On, off, on, off, on, off," he announces while she continues to confirm she sees nothing. Then the camera pans back to show the garage door of a house three doors down crashing up and down on the hood of his startled neighbor's car while he continues to chime, "On, off, on, off."[10]

Who can't see that life comes at you fast with lots of stuff? Stuff is my technical term for how relationships, achievement and focus change as you move through the various races of your life. Stuff happens as the seasons of life unfold, creating complexity that brings with it a seemingly endless battle of give and take for your time, energy and resources.

> "The art of being wise is the art of knowing what to discard."
> —William James

William James, known as the father of American psychology, said, "The art of being wise is the art of knowing what to discard."[11] The modern translation of James' advice is, "Get rid of stuff that does not matter." If you are investing time, talent and resources in relationships and activities that don't help you fulfill your commitment to the roles that matter most, get rid of them.

I met Danny DeArmas at a conference a couple years ago. He said something I will never forget. He said, "I don't make the rules, I just observe them." He was pointing to the fact that there are a lot of unwritten rules in life you shouldn't ignore. You don't have to like these rules. But the effect of these rules on performance and outcomes is real. They represent truths gained from extensive experience and observation. Choosing to ignore these unwritten rules leaves you to learn timeless lessons on your own and waste scarce time and resources. Or you can apply these rules and increase your rate of growth, improve personal performance and increase impact.

So here goes. I didn't make this rule—I just observe it and have experienced it. If you want to run a great race and finish strong, clarify in vivid detail your most important roles and the impact you want to have through them. Then focus on investing your time, energy and resources on fulfilling those roles—don't be distracted by unimportant stuff.

### *Confirming role clarity*

Clarifying and prioritizing your impact roles is hard. It requires thoughtful contemplation. Start by identifying all of the people, pursuits and activity that consumes your time. Imagine placing them all in a rowboat. You are the captain and your fully-loaded boat is quickly sinking. The only way to stay afloat is to throw stuff overboard. It won't be easy. The stuff in the boat represents who and what you are today. But to create the impact you envision, you'll need to throw stuff overboard that you may find hard to discard. Make no mistake...leaving behind what is comfortable and familiar is tough.

There is a scene in the movie *Captain and Commander* where Jack Aubrey and his crew are in a vicious and raging storm. A member of his crew has climbed up the mast to bring a sail down while the wind threatens to capsize the ship. Nearing a point where he is in danger of losing the ship and his entire crew, Aubrey orders another crew member to cut the sail loose. The decision will save the ship and its crew, but Captain Aubrey will send a man to his death. The sail is cut and the crewman is swept out to sea. Aubrey is overwhelmed with grief as a result of his gut-wrenching decision. But he made the decision, knowing that from loss a much larger victory would rise.

So, Captain, in no particular order, what are your five most important roles in life? These are the roles that provide you the most significant opportunities to impact the people you love, the teams you lead and the causes that stir your heart.

- _____
- _____
- _____
- _____
- _____

You will be on your way to clarity if you can say "yes" to this question: "If I focus on these five roles over the next year, does it provide me the greatest opportunity to maximize my personal impact?"

Was it hard to pick five?—it may have been difficult. Given the objective to increase your impact, let's raise the stakes. How would you prioritize your top five roles in order of importance and impact? The only way to assure clarity is to give priority to the roles that are most important.

Back to the rowboat. Which of the five roles would you throw out first? This role belongs on line five. Throw your roles out of the boat one at a time until you arrive at the role you would place on line one.

1. _____
2. _____
3. _____
4. _____
5. _____

Remember the example of the wheel in chapter five? The role you place in the center of the wheel (on the top line as number one) is going to be the lens through which you see and act on every other role in your life. Stephen Covey said, "Whatever is at the center of our life will be the source of our security, guidance, wisdom, and power."[12] This is where your love lies.

How would you feel if it was the only role left for you to pursue? I am not saying you wouldn't experience a sense of loss, disappointment or maybe even failure if the other roles were stripped away—you would. But whatever you put on the top line is your true north. It declares to the world what you think is the most important thing in your life.

Just a reminder—I don't make the rules. I just observe them.

### *Clarity meets reality*

In a "Calvin & Hobbes" comic strip, Calvin proudly announces that he has created the biggest snowball in the world, and he can't wait to "plaster" someone with it. Hobbes looks at the giant snowball and asks, "How are you going to pick it up?" Calvin falls to the ground in dismay and proclaims, "Reality continues to ruin my life."[13] A great plan foiled by reality.

Reality has a way of delivering a candid and sometimes harsh evaluation of your plans. Even if you ignore reality, it consistently returns an honest assessment of your position in the race. Who hasn't felt like Calvin? You think you are focused on your most important roles. Then, as you are confidently running, it is pointed out to you that you are not living up to your role commitments.

A great plan does not have to be ruined by reality. It just needs to be adjusted. Here are some assessment questions to get you back on track.

- If I focus on the five roles I identified as my highest priority roles, will the people I want to be most remembered by be positively and consistently impacted?
    - If the answer is no, what roles need to be added or deleted?
- If I were on the final lap of my final race, are there important people in my life to whom I would owe an apology? Who, if anyone, would be disappointed?
    - If the answer is yes, think about the impact you most desire to have with this person. Clearly the action you would take is different depending where this person fits into your life.
    - Are they important enough for you to consider adding an additional role to your list?
    - Is the impact you desire great enough to suggest you replace a role on your original priority list?
- Ask the people who are impacted by your role performance a couple questions.

- What do I need to do more of, less of, or stop doing to be more effective and impactful in this role?
- What is your greatest fear? The answer to this question provides valuable insights into their motivations, aspirations and thinking. When you know what the important people in your life fear, it will help you shape how you support them.

> "There are few
> things more
> powerful than
> a life lived with
> passionate clarity,"
> —Erwin McManus

"There are few things more powerful than a life lived with passionate clarity," says Erwin McManus, the author of *The Artisan Soul*. "We all need to create, to be a part of a process that brings to the world something beautiful, good, and true, in order to allow our souls to come to life."[14] Clarity is born out of simplicity and lends itself to focus. Focusing on your highest priority roles is the path to getting back on track and sustaining positive impact.

### Hook your goals to your impact roles

Goals make your roles come to life. To get back on track and revitalize your race, hook goals to your impact roles. In his book *Working Without A Net*, Morris Shechtman describes the rudderless nature your roles take on if you do not empower them with goals. "When we reach our destinations—when we achieve our goals we are the most vulnerable to failure. We become caught up in celebrating the achievement and neglect to reset new goals for ourselves. Without that resetting, chaotic feelings descend and push us toward safe, no-risk paths."[15]

Think of a time in your life when you accomplished a significant goal. What was your first thought? Right, let's celebrate! Most significant achievements do not signify the end of the race—they define a singular moment of impact on your way to the finish line.

I have a friend who is an accomplished marathon runner. He has run dozens of marathons, including the famed Boston Marathon. I asked Shawn about his race strategy. "When do you think about the finish line?" "I always see myself crossing the finish line," he said, "But I don't think about it when I am running. I break the race into sections, and set time goals for each of those check points." Lasting and sustaining impact is not an event. Impact is a journey that you live out through a process of setting and achieving checkpoint goals.

Marriage is certainly a journey. Years ago on a long flight home, the gentleman sitting next to me struck up a conversation. He had an interesting history of experiences and accomplishments. Noticing his wedding band, I asked him, "How long have you been married?" He smiled and replied, "35 years." "Wow," I said, "That's amazing. Congratulations!" "Yes, it truly is," he said in a tone that grabbed my attention. "And it is only my fourth wife," he added as he started to laugh.

Certainly a funny story, but four wives in 35 years is not how you'd envision marriage unfolding. Before my wife and I got married, I remember finishing up our pre-marriage counseling and asking Pastor Sam, "What is the key to a long marriage?" At the time Sam had been married, to the same woman, for nearly 30 years. He did not hesitate for a moment. His message was that marriage is a day-to-day commitment. Don't take it for granted. Success in marriage is measured over a lifetime, but the victory is earned day by day. Renew your commitment to growing together every day.

Races change, but the objective remains the same—how do you maximize your impact and finish strong. The key to getting on track, staying focused and breaking through the tape of a long and arduous race is not complex or sophisticated.

1. Design your race plan by breaking it down into relevant goals aligned with your highest priority roles.
2. Hook your race-advancing goals to each of your most important roles and renew your commitment to fulfilling them every day.

### Simply stick with it

In my experience of coaching impact principles, I have worked with a lot of high achievers. I've found few groups more driven than highly compensated and successful sales professionals. But even these rainmakers are not immune from getting off track. I work extensively with a very gifted young man when he gets stuck. Although he earns hundreds of thousands of dollars in annual compensation, he gets off track from time to time. When Shad gets stuck, my phone rings.

Shad has boundless energy and creativity. His incredible heart for his faith and family is always on display. Shad is always pursuing big projects and big dreams. When he calls, our conversation typically begins with me asking, "Tell me what is going on." In a matter of minutes Shad runs through dozens of ideas, projects and relationships he is pursuing. You could say Shad is a "just do it" guy.

Eventually he comes up for air. That's when I say, "Show me your plan." I am counting on Shad's predictable reply to set the stage for getting him back on track. His response will sound something like, "Jim, you know that is not my strength." Yes, I most certainly did. It always leads us back to role clarity and goal alignment—simplifying.

Steve Jobs, the founder of Apple, had this to say about power of simplicity, "That's been one of my mantras—focus and simplicity. Simple can be harder than complex: You have to work hard to get your thinking clean to make it simple. But it's worth it in the end because once you get there, you can move mountains." He's right—simple can be harder than complex.

Getting to simple is the path to getting back on track and staying on track. Employing a few key questions will help you:

- Clarify and focus on priority roles.
- Align short-term actions with your most critical and relevant goals.

*Question #1*: What are your five most important roles?

- Have they changed? Why or why not?
  - Have your role priorities changed? Why or why not?
  - Does your investment of time, energy and resources reflect your role priorities?
    - If not, what needs to change?

*Question #2*: What is the most important goal you should pursue to effect the greatest impact in each role? I am sure you can think of more than one goal. Keep your thinking simple and focused.

- In the next 30 days?
- In the next 90 days?
- In the next year?

*Question #3*: My greatest accomplishment in the next year will be? Think about the dreams you have packed into your possibility box.

|     | Role | Accomplishment |
| --- | --- | --- |
| 1. | _____ | _____ |
| 2. | _____ | _____ |
| 3. | _____ | _____ |
| 4. | _____ | _____ |
| 5. | _____ | _____ |

Simple, focused and executable. (See the appendix to get your free *Tape Breakers Impact Package*)

## Get Set—Connect to Your Source of Power

Imagine for a moment that you walk into your house and you hit the switch to turn on a light and nothing happens. Thinking the light bulb has burned out, you walk to another light switch and flip it—again no light. You look outside and see your neighbors' lights are on. For even a moment would you think the potential for light in your house was lost? Not even for a second.

You'd head to the main electrical panel and see the main electrical breaker to the house has been tripped. You reset the breaker and walk back into the house. Now you flip the light switch on and you have light.

The electrical potential in your home was never lost. But when the main source of electrical power is turned off, nothing works. You were created for a great purpose. You were designed to run a great race and deliver memorable impact. Potential never goes dormant. It just gets disconnected from its source of power. You slow down and run off track when you become disconnected from your source of power.

Your race is powered by answering a single, simple, yet complex question—"Why?" It is easy to identify a wish list of things you want—even figure out how you can get them. But what and how are like a light or appliance in your house. They do not come to life without power. Impact gets its power from answering "Why?"

> Motivation is not extraordinary, unusual or elusive when you identify who is positively impacted when you strive for excellence in the roles that truly matter.

Motivation is not extraordinary, unusual or elusive when you identify who is positively impacted when you strive for excellence in the roles that truly matter. Throughout history you see great impact emerge from a meaningful sense of why—it draws you into the stadium and propels you to the finish line. Michelangelo, one of the most influential and revered artists in history wrote, "The greatest danger for most of us is not that our aim is too high and we miss it, but that it is too low and we reach it."

### What is your life's blueprint?

Martin Luther King Jr. lived out his why every day. Dr. King understood the power of why—he had a dream. On October 26, 1967, he spoke to a group of students at Barrett Junior High School in Philadelphia. Dr. King asked them, "What is your life's blueprint?"

His words challenged them to connect to the power of why. "And when you discover what you will be in your life, set out to do it as if God Almighty called you at this particular moment in history to do it. Don't just set out to do a good job. Set out to do such a good job that the living, the dead or the unborn couldn't do it any better. If it falls your lot to be a street sweeper, sweep streets like Michelangelo painted pictures, sweep streets like Beethoven composed music, sweep streets like Leontyne Price sings before the Metropolitan Opera. Sweep streets like Shakespeare wrote poetry. Sweep streets so well that all the hosts of heaven and earth will have to pause and say: Here lived a great street sweeper who swept his job well."[16]

Impact flows freely, effectively and powerfully from hearts and minds alive with a full sense of why. Your race slows and becomes difficult when you are not connected to the power of why.

## Go! Commit to Build a Plan and Take Action

I have a friend who was focused on growing in his role as a young father. I suggested to Thomas that he sit down with his five-year-old son, Logan, and ask him what he would dream of doing in the next year. "What will happen," I said, "is that Logan will share some of his dreams with you. Those dreams will serve as goals you can work on together. Logan learns about achievement. You create a bond that allows you to grow in your role as a dad."

A few weeks after the conversation, Thomas sent me a picture of Logan's goals. They were written on a white board in Logan's room where they could both see them.

### Logan's 2015 Goals

1. See a live Zebra by June 1.
2. See a dinosaur bone exhibit by Sept. 30
3. Go see a big white Polar Bear by June 1.
4. Eat at Chipotle 5 times.

Remember there is power in simplicity. You'll get back on track by constructing specific written goals for each of your five top prioritized roles. Written goals supported with action plans have been shown to raise goal achievement by nearly 50%.[17]

### *Eight proven steps to achieve your goals*

In a 2007 study, by Professor Richard Wiseman, of 3,000 people attempting to achieve a range of resolutions, only 12% actually achieved their goals.[18] In a 2014 study by the University of Scranton, only 8% achieved their goals and 49% produced infrequent success.[19] Research consistently reveals goal achievement is a fleeting pursuit.

The principal reason we do not reach goals, regardless of their impact and meaning, is a failure to execute a proven process in a disciplined manner. Achievement leaves clues. Study those who demonstrate a consistent pattern of achievement and you find that they have executed a proven recipe of success. Regardless of the size, complexity or timeframe of the goal, the application of these steps has proven to produce consistent results.

Think through these steps, thinking about what you identified as your greatest accomplishment in your top-priority role.

Step #1: State your goal—be specific.
Step #2: What benefits or impact will result from the achievement of this goal?
Step #3: What date will you accomplish this goal by?
Step #4: Identify the skills and knowledge you will need to acquire to achieve this goal.
Step #5: Identify who can help? (teachers, coaches, organizations, associations, websites).
Step #6: Identify the obstacles and challenges you anticipate.
Step #7: Identify the investment required. What will it cost?
Step #8: Build a plan of action taking into consideration your date and identified needs and opportunities.

## Don't let obstacles get in your way

St. Petersburg, Russia, was the vision of Peter the Great. He envisioned St. Petersburg as a showcase of imperial splendor and the centerpiece of his new vision for the country. Even before the first shovel of dirt was turned, this 18th century city was completely planned out.

To accommodate the plan, numerous large rocks had to be removed. There was one particularly large boulder that was right in the middle of a major avenue. The administrators solicited bids for its removal. Because modern equipment and explosives did not exist, the bids were too high. As the official wondered what to do, a peasant presented himself and offered to get rid of the boulder for a much lower price than the other bidders. Having nothing to lose, they gave him the job.

The next day the peasant showed up with a small army of other peasants carrying shovels. Right next to the rock they dug a huge hole much larger than the size of the boulder. They then pushed the boulder into the hole, covered everything up, and carted off the extra dirt.

Everyone gets off track. Everyone gets lost. Albert Einstein said, "You cannot solve a problem using the same level or basis of thought used to create it." Remember being lost is a situation and not a permanent condition. Just take a step back and assess your race position. On your mark—clarify your roles and goals. Get set—connect with your why. Go—retool your plan and take action.

See you at the finish line!

# PART 4

## Finishing Strong

### "Breaking the Tape and Standing on the Podium"

> *"In the end, it's not the years in your life that count. It's the life in your years."*
> —ABRAHAM LINCOLN

> *"It is not the end of the physical body that should worry us. Rather, our concern must be to live while we're alive."*
> —ELISABETH KÜBLER-ROSS

# CHAPTER 15

# Breaking the Tape: "Standing on the Podium"

*"When I stand before God at the end of my life, I would hope*
*that I would not have a single bit of talent left, and could say, 'I*
*used everything you gave me."*
—ERMA BOMBECK

In 1992, I boarded an Orange County flight to San Francisco on my way
to an evening speaking engagement. We rolled down the runway for a
routine southernly takeoff. Just as routinely, I tipped my seat back and
closed my eyes. As we climbed steeply out over the Pacific Ocean, I began
to mentally rehearse my presentation. But not for long.

I immediately sat up and looked out the window when the pilot banked
quickly to the left. I immediately thought, "Why wasn't he following the
normal pattern of slowly easing to the right and heading north?" The
answer was about to turn my quick 60-minute flight into anything but
routine.

We were flying slowly down the coastline towards San Diego when the
pilot came on and abruptly asked the flight attendants to remain seated.
The beautiful ocean view disappeared as we turned inland. The pilot announced that we were returning to the Orange County airport, and soon
we were stacked into the landing pattern. As we approached the runway,
something wasn't right.

I had landed at the Orange County airport hundreds of times and couldn't figure out why we were flying so much higher than normal as we approached the airport. Spotting familiar landmarks, it was obvious we were in for another surprise. Seemingly just a few hundred feet above the runway, we buzzed the tower and climbed back out over the ocean. Again we banked to the left. I didn't know what was going on, but I knew you don't do a fly-by over Newport Beach for fun.

Now slowly circling Catalina Island, the pilot's first words after "Ladies and Gentlemen" were "Don't be alarmed." After those comforting words, he told us the landing gear on the plane did not detract properly after take-off. At this point, most everyone skipped right over alarmed and went to panicked. He informed us that the crew would be moving about the cabin going through a procedural checklist to fix the malfunction and asked everyone to stay seated.

The crew urgently scurried around the cabin. They pulled up carpet and opened up floor panels as we continued to circle over Catalina Island. After what seemed like an eternity, the pilot came back on the intercom to alarm us with the news that they were unable to fix the problem. The technical explanation was that the landing gear partially retracted and they could not manually or electronically get it to move. Uncertain about how the landing gear would react upon landing, the pilot announced that we would prepare for an emergency landing at Los Angeles International Airport (LAX).

Flight crews are well trained, but all the training in the world can't simulate an actual crash landing. Flight attendants pulled down manuals they likely only reviewed in a simulator. As they ruffled through the pages, you could sense we were entering uncharted territory. It was evident no one knew what to expect, not even the pilots.

Based on the visual inspection of the landing gear, the pilots believed the landing gear would collapse upon landing. Everyone could complete the picture of what that meant without further explanation. In preparation, we would circle offshore and burn all excess fuel while ground crews at LAX prepared emergency resources for our attempted landing. As the plane circled off the coast of Long Beach, the flight attendants did their best to keep people calm. It was going to take up to an hour to burn the fuel down, so we had plenty of time for our minds to run wild. The lady seated next to me asked if she could hold my hand, and I did my best to calm her nerves. I don't think there was anyone on the plane who didn't consider that this could be their final race.

I was in the prime of my racing life. There was so much more for me to do, so many unfinished races. I pulled out a pad of paper and wrote letters to my wife and sons. I wrote feverishly. I tried to cram a lifetime of knowledge, experience, thoughts and apologies into those letters. I was overwhelmed by the urgency of the moment. I was grasping for anything to help me push down the fear rising within me. If you have had one of these life moments, you know what I mean. I understood life comes to an end, but not today!

I had plenty of time to replay my entire life before the pilot announced he had permission to land. As the plane turned towards land, my heart began beating faster. The flight attendants began calling out instructions. As the plane banked left towards LAX, the uncertainty was nearly suffocating. I struggled to catch my breath. I rose up to get some air and looked out of the window. It looked like a scene out of a movie. The runway was covered in fire-retardant foam. The lights from the long line of emergency vehicles pierced through the haze.

Time seemed to stand still. It felt like the plane was moving so slowly we would fall out of the sky. Anxious passengers kept popping their heads up to peek out the windows while the flight attendant streamed a steady course of, "For your safety and the safety of those around you, please keep your head tucked forward between your knees." Then in the flash of a moment it sounded like the engines died and we heard a thunderous clapping sound as the wheels hit the runway. My body tightened as I braced for the unexpected—this is it!

Nothing immediately happened. I felt the plane coasting down the runway and looked out the window. Foam, kicked up upon contact, streamed down over the windows—we're safe. Was the clapping sound the landing gear snapping to attention? It didn't matter what happened, how it happened, or why it happened. I think I just unwrapped a miracle. I don't remember any of the announcements made after we touched down. All I could think about was how close I felt to the end of my race. Wouldn't you?

When we stepped off the jetway, into the terminal, there were dozens of television cameras and reporters there to greet us. In a sea of bright lights, airline officials tried to scurry us off to a meeting room while reporters shouted out questions. I heard someone ask, "How do you feel?" It wasn't directed at me, but I can tell you exactly how I felt.

## The Meaning of Life

Nothing feels normal when the finish line prematurely comes into view. You look back over your life, and you don't think about what you've done... you think about what you've left undone. You don't think about who you've served...you think about who you failed to serve. You don't think about your next promotion, raise or accomplishment. What you do think about is who you've become. You think about the people you'd miss and the people who would miss you.

Looking at the finish line feels like playing a part in a movie, only to realize you're not acting—it's real. Dr. Timothy Johnson, a Senior Medical Contributor for ABC News, describes this feeling, writing, "Part of the pleasure of reading a novel lies in not knowing how it will turn out until we get to the last page—and then thinking back to how the characters might have lived differently had they known what the end would be like. But real life has an urgency so different from fiction; at the end, it cannot be changed! 'The meaning of life is that it stops.' We will never figure out how we should live our life unless we fully understand the significance of the fact that it will end. And then what?"[1]

Real life is lived out by pursuing impact. Impact injects urgency into your plans and connects you with people. Impact defines your motivation to achieve. It is the energy that breaths life into your race. Impact embodies a purpose so energizing that it blocks out pain. It proudly wears the scars from failure as badges of courage won in the pursuit of running and finishing well.

No one knows how many races you will run on your way to the finish line, what the conditions will be like, how events will unfold in your life, or how these events will affect your roles. But your race tells the story of how you used your time, talent and resources to pursue lasting impact—positively changing lives.

## You Were Created To Do Great Things

The importance of impact was awakened in me by George Raveling. George is one of the great college basketball coaches in history. During his tenure as the head basketball coach at Washington State University, he hosted a summer basketball camp that was attended by thousands of junior high and high school kids. They came to hone their basketball skills, but George would send them away thinking about impact.

On the last day of camp all of the campers gathered in the bleachers of Bohler Gymnasium. The buzz and chatter turned to near-deafening silence when George walked in. No need to call everyone to attention or introduce Coach Raveling. Standing 6'7" tall, George was a bigger-than-life action figure. He consistently flashed a warm and engaging smile. George capably projected a captivating presence across any room.

He began walking back and forth in front of the bleachers until every eye was focused on him. Coach Raveling wove stories of life and basketball together with untempered passion and enthusiasm. He made us laugh, but most of all he made us think. We left, believing we were created for a great purpose—to live a life of impact.

At the end, Coach Raveling stood center court at the base of the bleachers. Standing tall, feet firmly planted on the ground, he began to raise his arm above his head. He raised his eyes to look at the palm of his hand, facing the ground, above his head. Then scanning across the bleachers, he said, "My greatest fear is to stand before God and have him tell me, George, I gave you this much ability," as he again looked up at the palm of his hand towering above the floor. "But George, you only used this much of it," now lowering his hand down to his waist. "You could have done so much more and been so much more. I equipped you with the tools. All you had to do was try." Then Coach Raveling raised his hand back above his head. He glanced at his hand and then back at us. Then, with unbridled passion and enthusiasm, he told us we possessed unmistakable talent and we were created to do great things. George encouraged us to pursue our dreams. He pressed us to run with the purpose of delivering lasting impact.

Impact is about breaking the tape—finishing strong. Breaking the tape and simply finishing the race are as different as night and day. It's the difference between muddling through the day in anxious anticipation that tomorrow may somehow be magically different and making an intentional decision to create lasting impact.

Tape breakers run through the tape welcoming the next race while leaving nothing undone behind them. A friend described *breaking the tape* perfectly. While coaching a young girls' softball team, he always stressed to the girls "don't run *to* first base; run *through* first base. With an expanded vision of the goal, they ran harder, faster and with more conviction.

Tape breakers race to hear "well done" when they cross the finish line. They don't concern themselves with commemorative pictures, 15 minutes of fleeting fame, or a victory lap. Tape breakers nurture the seeds of impact, enabling them to write a story of hope and opportunity on the hearts of the people they meet over the course of their race.

## A Few Final Racing Thoughts

*Race with urgency*. Impact is synonymous with urgency. To realize the full extent of your potential for impact, you must adopt the mindset of urgency. The Psalmist wrote, "Teach us to number our days, that we may gain a heart of wisdom."[2] Thirty is not the new 20 anymore than 40 is the new 30, or any season of life is on hold, recovered or lost by simply wrapping it up in a cliche. Impact does not show up in the mail as an invitation. It is within your reach every day begging to be seized.

*Get success right.* Your most important roles define who you are and what is important to you. They will lead you towards lasting impact. Success is the identification of your most important roles, values and goals, and living your personal and professional life in alignment with your chosen roles, values and goals.

*Get started*. You'll never be fully prepared for any race. If you wait to get started you'll miss important opportunities. Look for the second curve and start new races. Accept the challenge to begin anew and start new races. The joy and challenge is in the journey.

*Allow yourself to be surprised.* Planning is important, even essential. But don't allow your plan to rob you of vision and creativity.

*Sometimes all you can do is take the next step.* You can only control what you can control. Anytime you are stuck ask yourself, "Is what I am doing right now contributing to my highest priority roles and goals?" Take the next step.

*Don't dwell on defeat or disappointment too long.* You aren't going to win every race. You don't have to like losing, but you do have to get over it. Those who fail to move on grow bitter and fail to mentally prepare themselves to start new races. Ben Stein frames it up saying, "It is inevitable that some defeat will enter even the most victorious life. The human spirit is never finished when it is defeated...it is finished when it surrenders." Keep moving.

*Know what you stand for.* Pursue truth and grow deep in your knowledge and understanding of timeless principles and values. When you lose sight of who you are it makes you vulnerable to being pulled off course. When you know yourself and stay true to yourself you'll be running on an unshakable foundation.

*Think in can's.* Did, won't, might, can't, ought, try, will and can. Common words but words of implicit and powerful meaning. *Did* is a word of achievement. *Won't* is a word of retreat. *Might* is a word of indifference. *Can't* is a word of defeat. *Ought* is a word of duty. *Try* is a word of effort. *Will* is a word of commitment. *Can* is a word of power. Think in can's—they are filled with effort and energy that produce results.

## One Final Question

I am convinced that deep within every one of us is a burning desire to live impactful lives that result in powerfully and positively changing lives. Impact is not an accidental journey. Impact is a conscious choice to love, equip and serve. There is not a particular season of life designated to pursue impact. We don't miss the opportunity for impact due to our age, circumstance or condition. We miss the opportunity for impact simply by failing to choose it.

Neil Cavuto said, "Rich and poor. Powerful and not so powerful. We all come into this world, and we all leave it. It's what we do in between that defines and motivates us. He's right. Your race lies between. This is the time you have to become you. In our youth we think we have unlimited time and may pay little attention to our direction or destination—we have plenty of time to figure it out. As we grow older, we look back and wonder where the time went to, wishing we had figured it out sooner.

Life has a way of absorbing us into its natural and inevitable progression to the finish line. As life picks up momentum, we adapt to the myriad of changing circumstances and conditions. In what seems like the blink of an eye, once too young becomes now too old. But the question at the finish line will remain the same, "Why didn't you become you?"

I once heard a story about a Harvard law graduate going to the office of his favorite professor to thank him and say good-bye. The professor greeted him warmly when he entered his office. They enjoyed recounting their experiences from the past three years. As he was about to leave, the professor asked him, "What are you going to do now?" He replied, "Study and pass the bar." "And then what?" the professor asked. Excitedly, he replied, "I am going to go to work for one of the most prestigious law firms in NYC!" "Wonderful," the professor said, "and then what?" "Well, then I hope to become a partner," the prized student replied. "Well, that would be a great accomplishment. I think you will make it," the professor offered.

The professor continued to probe, "What are your plans after making partner?" "My goal is to become a Supreme Court Justice," he proudly announced. The professor, effusing encouragement, replied, "Wouldn't that be amazing? I can see you aspiring to the highest court in the land. And then what?" The young man, now thinking about the personal nature of the professor's question, replied, "I hope to get married, raise a family, build a vacation home on the beach, and retire." The professor nodded acknowledgement, smiled and replied, "and then what?"

At this moment the young man realized the wise professor was asking him whether his choices would produce impact. Succeeding at things that truly matter. Changing lives forever! Our mind once challenged with a question never retreat to its previous state. A seemingly simple and innocuous question should command our full attention—And then what?

It is never too early, or too late, to choose impact. Start each day picturing the end of your race. See yourself entering the stadium. Stop running for a moment. Stand still and look up into the stands. Picture the people you want to be remembered by, the people whose lives you want to positively change, the people you don't want to disappoint. Now think about your day and ask, "Is what I am choosing to pursue today serving these people in my life?"

On your mark! Get set! Go!

Run through the tape. Your physical strength and vibrancy will ebb and flow, but as long as you possess life, your most important step is your next step. Some of the greatest victories in history were born out of taking the next step in seemingly insignificant moments. You don't have to be strong—you just need to be committed. The best you will consistently pour out when you use your time, talent and resources pursuing impact.

Worldly success will tempt you—don't fall into the trap.

New possibilities will rise up within you—act on them.

Seasons will change—keep running.

Circumstances will challenge you—keep running.

Adversity will strike—stand tall.

Temptations will distract you—don't run alone.

No one has your unique place in history to positively impact the people you love, the teams you lead and the causes that stir your heart the way you do. You were designed and created for impact.

Every day is another page in the story of your race—don't squander a single moment of it. This is an opportunity for impact that has your name written on it. No one can run the race you were created to run. Run a race that weaves together a story bold enough and big enough to change lives, inspire hearts and unlock possibilities.

Be a *Tape Breaker*. So when you are asked at that precious moment, "Why didn't you become you," you'll have run a race filled with lasting impact.

# Acknowledgements

### MY WIFE

Thank you Kristi for your love, encouragement, and support. There is no way to thank you for all you have done and continue to do to enrich my life and the life of our family. Your heart for service consistently shines a bright light on what an impactful race should look like.

### MY MOM AND DAD

Thank you for setting the example and showing that real personal impact is a state of mind and condition of our heart that moves us to love and serve.

### MY FAMILY

Matthew, Andrew, Johnny, Nicholas, Katherine, and Kathleen; you helped me figure out what impact really means. Thanks for all you have done to enrich my race. Debbie and Bob, thanks for being there every step along the way.

### MY COACHES, MENTORS, AND CONFIDANTS

Thank you for your prayers, support and the countless ways you have helped me along the way.

Bob Akers, George Ayrouth, Ron Bridges, Bruce Carson, Tom Coss, Butch Ferguson, Charlie Griener, Bill Harper, John Heinaman, Jerry Howells, Jim Ireland, Tom Kadien, Rich Lowe, Roland Lyson, Perry Lyson, Stan Lyson, Joe MacKrell, Bill Milligan, Kary Oberbrunner, Kevin Pearce, Tom Phelps, Bruce Tollner, John Torrey, Brian Rodgers, Walt Sebring, Craig Shugert, Larry Stillman, John Steward, Jim Suski, and Peter Vanderhyden.

## MY READERS, EDITORS, AND TRUTH TELLERS

Thank you for the feedback and assistance to make this project better.

Debbie Akers, Matthew Akers, Carrie Barrett, Ed Garrison, Patty Lyson-Green, Jessie Paine, David Peterson, Thomas Osthus, Mark Samuels, Shad Smith, Terry Taber, Josh Taylor, Rod Tamura, Terrie Squire, and Shirley Werner

## MY FRIENDS

Thank you to the many people I had the pleasure to work with through the years. Your impact on my life is immeasurable and you helped create and shape so many of the incredible experiences I enjoyed over the course of my career. You know who you are—thanks for staying in touch.

# Appendix

# I'd love to help give your race a boost!

Raise your impact. Revitalize your plan to finish strong.

---

You are the only one who can positively impact the people you love, teams you lead and causes that stir your heart.

Let me help you build a great race plan.

In 60 minutes, I'll show you how to build a personalized plan designed to maximize your impact with the people you love, teams you lead and causes that stir your heart!

Just go to the link below and I'll send it to you.

> **Get it here:**
> http://bit.ly/TapeBreakers-
> GettingBackonTrack

# Tape Breaker Impact Package

Tools to revitalize your dreams, refresh your race and finish strong

The impact package has been created to help you become the "Tape Breaker" you were born to become.

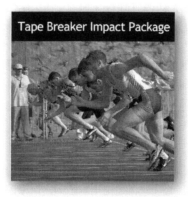

The "Impact Package" includes tools and resources to:

- Pump up your possibility box.
- Build plans proven to help you achieve your dreams.
- Organize your time, talent and energy around the roles and goals that truly matter—every day

We'd love to help you build a great race plan. Put these "Tape Breaker" strategies to work today. Go to the link below and get started on raising your impact and influence.

Get it here:
http://bit.ly/TapeBreakers-
ImpactPackage

# NOTES

## Chapter One: Life is all About Impact: "An Unlikely Source of Clarity

1. Chip Ingram, *Good to Great in Goods Eyes*, (Baker Books, Grand Rapids, MI, 2007), 39.

## Chapter Two: It's a Trap: "Looking for the Starting Line in all the Wrong Places"

1. D. Bruce Lockerbie, *Thinking and Acting Like a Christian* (Portland, OR: Multnomah Press, 1989), 51-52.

2. Alice in Wonderland, *Quotes*, <http://www.alice-in-wonderland.net/resources/chapters-script/alice-in-wonderland-quotes/> (1 October 2015).

3. Peggy Drexler, *How Women Define Success*, 22 July 2014, <http://www.forbes.com/sites/peggydrexler/2014/07/22/how-women-define-success/> (8 July 2015).

4. Business Wire, *New City/LinkedIn Survey*, 28 October 2014, <http://www.businesswire.com/news/home/20141028005207/en/CitiLinkedIn-Survey-Reveals-Men-Struggle-Work-Life-Balance> (8 July 2015).

5. Tony Campollo, *The Success Fantasy*, (Wheaton, IL: Victor Publishing, 1985), 9.

6. Race to Nowhere, *About the Film*, <http://www.racetonowhere.com/about-film> (27 April 2015).

## Chapter Three: Finding the Starting Line: "Choose Well"

1. Out There Monthly, *Was This Man Cheated Out Of An Olympic Medal? Don Kardong and the strange case of East German Athletics*, (1 March 2011)

<http://www.outtheremonthly.com/was-this-man-cheated-out-of-an-olympic-medal-don-kardong-and-the-strange-case-of-east-german-athletics/> (4 April 2015).

2. The Legend, *Winning the Lydiard way the top coach Barry Magee*, <http://thelegend.co.nz/barry_magee.php> (5 April 2015).

3. AZ Quotes, *Barry MaGee*, <http://thinkexist.com/quotation/anyone-can-run-miles-it-s-the-next-six-that-count/1188281.html> (5 April 2015).

4. Jordan Weissmann, *Here's Exactly How Many College Graduates Live Back at Home*, (26 February 2013), <http://www.theatlantic.com/business/archive/2013/02/heres-exactly-how-many-college-graduates-live-back-at-home/273529/> (5 April 2015).

5. Charles Handy, *The Age of Paradox*, (Boston, MA: Harvard University Press,1994), 50-51.

6. Paulo Coelho, *The Zahir*, (HarperCollins e-books; Reprint edition (October 13, 2009)

7. Charles Handy, *The Age of Paradox*, (Boston, MA: Harvard University Press,1994), 54.

8. Active Editors, *10 Biggest Running Races in the U.S.*, *<http://www.active.com/running/articles/10-biggest-running-races-in-the-u-s>* (28 September 2015).

9. SB Nation, *The history of 'I'm going to Disney World!' at the Super Bowl*, (2 February 2014) <http://www.sbnation.com/nfl/2014/2/2/5363088/going-to-disney-world-super-bowl-history> (30 March 2015).

**Chapter Four: Be Rich Towards What Counts: "Real Wealth Starts with a Question"**

1. Aly Taylor, *Cancer Made Me a Mommy*, (Monroe, LA, Aly's Fight, 2015), 12.

2. The Phrase Finder, *Time and tide wait for no one*, <http://www.phrases.org.uk/meanings/384000.html> (11 April 2015).

3. Lee Eisenberg, *The Number,* (New York, New York, Simon & Schuster, Inc., 2006), 249.

4. Richard Davis, *Because the Answers Have Changed*, (10 February 2013), <http://www.rkndavis.com/business-technology/because-the-answers-have-changed/> (16 September 2015).

5. Editors of Perseus Publishing, *Movers and Shakers: the 100 Most Influential Figures in Modern Business*, (New York, NY: Perseus Publishing, 2003), 205-207.

6. Andy Grove, *Swimming Across: A Memoir*, (New York, NY: Grand Central Publishing, 2002), 229.

**Chapter Five: Don't Be Disappointed: "You've Got to Get This Right"**

1. *When E.F. Hutton talks, people listen, vintage tv commercial -YouTube*. On line video clip, <https://www.youtube.com/watch?v=2MXqb1a3Apg> (5 May 2015).

2. Hodges, Chris (2012-09-04). Fresh Air: Trading Stale Spiritual Obligation for a Life-Altering, Energizing, Experience-It-Everyday Relationship with God (p. 111). Tyndale House Publishers. Kindle Edition.

3. Keith Sharon, *Turning his life around: Former Tesoro High star quarterback went from heroin addict to his mom calling the cops on him*, Orange County Register on the web, 9 September 2015, <http://www.ocregister.com/articles/nick-684073-rick-nelson.html> (12 September 2015).

4. Ibid.

## Chapter Six: Possibilities: "How Big is Your Box?"

1. Rob Wallace and Steve Schnee, *ABC News*, 23 December, 2009, <http://abcnews.go.com/2020/BlindSide/blind-side-michael-oher-story/story?id=9390739> (1 October 2015)

2. Josh Levin, *Slate*, 14 October 2010, <http://www.slate.com/articles/sports/sports_nut/2010/10/the_other_blind_sides.html> (1 October 2015).

3. Ibid.

4. PBS.com Editors, *T. E. Lawrence, Laurence of Arabia*,<http://www.pbs.org/lawrenceofarabia/players/lawrence2.html> (1 October 2015)

5. Rejoinder, *Clapway*, 30 May 2015, <http://clapway.com/2015/05/30/92-year-old-runner-vows-to-run-historic-race123/> (1 October 2015)

6. Ibid.

7. Hezekiah Butterworth, *The Great Composers* (Boston: D. Lathrop and Company, 1884), 47.

8. Andy Andrews, *The Final Summit*, (Nashville, TN: Thomas Nelson Publishing, 2010), 87.

## Chapter Seven: Don't Sit Out: "Developing the Courage to Run"

1. M. Scott Peck, *The Road Less Traveled and Beyond*, (New York, NY: Simon & Schuster Inc., 1997), 127-128.

2. 2. Bronnie Ware, *Regrets of the Dying*, 19 November 2009, <http://bronnieware.com/regrets-of-the-dying/> (1 October 2015).

3. Kim, *Increase Your Encouragement Quotient*, 12 February 2013, <http://redrockbiblecamp.com/increase-your-encouragement-quotient/> (22 August 2014).

4. Gabriel Hunt, *The Essential Abraham Lincoln* (New York, NY: Random House, 1993), 336.

5. John F. Kennedy, *Profiles in Courage,* (New York, NY: Easton Press, 1992), 137.

6. Amy Cuddy, *Your Body Shapes Who You Are,* (1 October 2012) <https://www.ted.com/speakers/amy_cuddy> (7 July 2014).

7. Christine Brennan, *Zach Johnson takes his place in history with Masters, British Open wins*, USA Today on the Web, 21 July 2015.

8. Zach Johnson, *About Zach, <http://zachjohnsongolf.com/ContentPages/Biography.aspx>* (24 July 2015).

9. Sarah Green, *Harvard Business Review*, 12 January 2012 <https://hbr.org/2012/01/the-right-mindset-for-success/> (21 February 2014).

10. Ibid.

11. Bob Buford, *Finishing Well*, (Nashville, TN: Integrity Publishers, 2004), 212-213.

**Chapter Eight: Practice: "Yes, We Are Going to Talk About Practice"**

1. Genius Sports, *"Practice" Press Conference*, 3 May 2002, <http://genius.com/Allen-iverson-practice-press-conference-annotated> (24 July 2015).

2. Shaw Sports editors, *The Players' Awards*, 21 July 2015, <http://shawsports.net/the-good-the-bad-and-the-questionable-from-the-players-awards/> (24 July 2015).

3. Bill Katovsky, *1,001 Pearls of Runners Wisdom* (New York, NY: Skyhorse Publishing, 2012).

4.  Franklin Steele, Bleacher Report, *Ranking the 10 Best NHL season by a Player Over 40 Years Old*, 12 November 2013, <http://bleacherreport.com/articles/1847225> (15 December 2013).

5.  Geoff Colvin, *Talent is Overrated* (New York, NY: Penguin Publishing, 2008), 7.

6.  Wanda Wilk, Polish Music Center at USC Education, *Polish Composers, Ignacy Jan Paderewski*, (1 November 2010). <http://www.usc.edu/dept/polish_music/composer/paderewski.html> (7 July 2015).

7.  Charles Phillips, *Paderewski The Story of a Modern Immortal*, (New York, NY: The MacMillan Company, 1934), 28.

8.  K. Anders Ericsoon, Michael J. Prietula, and Edward T. Cokely, *The Making of an Expert*, Harvard Business Review (July/August 2007).

9.  Vince Grippi, *Sandberg led quietly*, The Spokesman Review on Web 5 January 2005, <http://www.spokesman.com/stories/2005/jan/05/sandberg-led-quietly/> (2 August 2015)

10. K. Anders Ericsoon, Michael J. Prietula, and Edward T. Cokely, *The Making of an Expert*, Harvard Business Review (July/August 2007).

11. Ibid.

12. Ibid.

13. Wanda Wilk, Polish Music Center at USC Education, *Polish Composers, Ignacy Jan Paderewski*, (1 November 2010) <http://www.usc.edu/dept/polish_music/composer/paderewski.html> (7 July 2015).

14. Idid.

15. Editors, Paderewski Festival, *Ignacy Paderewski*, (1 January 2015) <http://www.paderewskifest.com/ignacy-paderewski/> (28 July 2015).

**Chapter Nine: "Who's Your Coach? - "The Secret to Great Preparation"**

1. A Better Perspective, *Hear what Global Leaders and the Media have to say about the Power of Coaching*, <http://www.abetterperspective.com/Quotes.html> (1 October 2015).

2. Ibid.

3. Frosty Westering, *Make The Big Time Where You Are* (Tacoma, WA: Big Five Productions, 1990), 34.

4. Ibid, 34.

5. Pacific Lutheran University editors, *Frosty Westering*, <http://golutes.com/sports/fball/frosty/frosty> (30 July 2015).

6. Marcus Buckingham, *The One Thing You Need to Know* (New York, NY: Simon & Schuster, 2005), 55.

7. Jason Selk, *10-Minute Toughness* (New York, NY: McGraw-Hill, 2009), 17.

8. John Maxwell, *Talent is Never Enough*, (Nashville, TN: Thomas Nelson Publishing, 2007), 7.

9. Brandon Specktor, Readers Digest, *What If Mozart Was Your Life Coach*, <http://www.rd.com/funny-stuff/mozart-life-lessons/> (31 July 2015).

10. Alison J. Head and Michael B. Eisenberg, First Monday, *How college students use the web to conduct everyday life research* (4 April 2011), *<http://firstmonday.org/article/view/3484/2857> (29 July 2015).*

11. Rob Carnevale, indieLondon, *Walk The Line - Reese Witherspoon Interview, (1 December 2015), <http://www.indielondon.co.uk/Film-Review/walk-the-line-reese-witherspoon-interview> (1 August 2015).*

12. Geoffrey L. Cohen, David Scott Yeager, Julio Garcia, Patti Brzustoski, William t. Hessert, Valerie Purdi-Vaughns, Nancy Apfel, Allison Master, and Matthew E. Williams, "Breaking the Cycle of Mistrust: Wise Interventions to Provide Critical Feedback Across the Racial Divide", *Journal of Experimental Psychology: General*, Vol 143, No. 2 (2014): 804-824.

13. Art Theil, *PLU Football Great Frosty Westering (1927-2013)*, Sports Press NW on the Web (4 April 2013), <http://sportspressnw.com/2149182/2013/plu-football-great-frosty-westering-1927-2013> (4 April 2013).

14. Art Theil, *Frosty, A Man No One Could Forget*, Sports Press NW on the Web (4 May 2013), <http://sportspressnw.com/2150837/2013/> (30 July 2015).

**Chapter Ten: Commitment: "Staying in Your Lane"**

1. IMS LLC, *Starting Grid Indianapolis 500 - 1975*, (20 May 1975) <https://www.indianapolismotorspeedway.com/events/indy500/history/historical-stats/race-stats/starting-grids/1975> (20 August 2015).

2. George Martin, "1975 Tom Sneva Indy Crash" YouTube. On line video clip, <https://www.youtube.com/watch?v=i4TO3NatTmY> (20 August 2015)

3. Viktor E. Frankl, *Man's Search for Meaning* (New York: Pocket Books, 1963), 104-105,

4. Ibid.

5. Barry Schwartz, *The Paradox of Choice*, (New York, Harper-Collins, 2009), ebook, x.

6. Barry Schwartz, *Can There Ever Be Too Many Flowers Blooming?*, PDF, Swarthmore College, pg. 13.

7. Ibid.

8. Nakia Melecio, *Courage to Stand on the Stage of Life*, (New York, NY: Lulu Publishing, 2014), 58.

9. Urban Dictionary, *stay in your lane*, (28 January 2007), <http://www.urbandictionary.com/define.php?term=stay+in+your+lane> (5 August 2015).

10. Neil Baldwin, *Edison, Inventing the Century*, (New York, NY: Hyperion, 1995), 409.

11. Gail Sheehy, *Pathfinders*, (New York, NY: Bantam Doubleday Dell, 1983).

12. Harold Myra, *The Leadership Secrets of Billy Graham*, (Grand Rapids, MI: Zondervan), 286.

13. Stacy Perman, *The Story of In-N-Out Burger*, (New York, NY: HarperCollins, 2009), 47.

14. Proverbs 29:18, NIV.

15. The Energy Project, *Company Profile*, (PDF), <http://theenergyproject.com/pdfs/TEP_brochure_11_13_13.pdffoo> (7 August 2015).

16. A. H. Maslow, *The Farther Reaches of Human Nature*, (New York, NY: Penguin Books, 1971), 35-37.

**Chapter Eleven: Accountability: "Never Run Alone"**

1. Ecclesiastes 4:9-10 NIV

2. J. Martin Kohe, *The Power to Choose*, (The Napoleon Hill Foundation, 2011), 12.

3. Chuck Swindoll, *Living Above the Level of Mediocrity*, (Waco, TX: Word Books, 1987), 133.

4. Randy Pausch, *The Last Lecture*, (New York, NY, 2008), 36-37.

5. Michael W. Chapman, *Gallup: Billy Graham Among 10 Most Admired Men in the World—for the 58th Time*, 30 December 2014, <http://www.cnsnews.com/news/article/michael-w-chapman/gallup-billy-graham-among-10-most-admired-men-world-58th-time> (7 October 2015).

6. Harold Myra, *The Leadership Secrets of Billy Graham*, (Grand Rapids, MI: Zondervan), 57-57.

7. Harold Myra, *The Leadership Secrets of Billy Graham*, (Grand Rapids, MI: Zondervan), 60.

8. Chuck Coonradt, *The Game of Work*, (Salt Lake City, UT: Liberty Press, 1991), 30.

9. Gail Matthews, *Study Focuses on Strategies for Achieving Goals, Resolutions*, 5 September 2008, <http://www.dominican.edu/dominicannews/study-highlights-strategies-for-achieving-goals> (11 November 2013).

10. Dallas Willard, *The Great Omission*, (New York, NY: Harper-Collins, 2009), 48.

11. The qualities of accountability were adapted from work by Chuck Swindoll, *Living Above the Level of Mediocrity*, (Waco, TX: Word Books, 1987) and Patrick Morley.

## Chapter Twelve: Balance: "So Many Races, So Little Time"

1. Harold Myra, *The Leadership Secrets of Billy Graham*, (Grand Rapids, MI: Zondervan), 60.

2.  Heidi Halvorson, *Succeed: How We Can Reach Our Goals*, (New York, NY: Penguin Group, 2011), 41.

3.  Wynn Davis, *The Best of Success* (New York: NY, Celebrating Excellence, 1989) BS27.

4.  W Mitchell, *It's Not What Happens to You, It's What You Do About It* (Colorado: Phoenix Press, 2001), xii.

5.  Nobel Prize Editors, *Albert Schweitzer*, <http://www.nobelprize. org/nobel_prizes/peace/laureates/1952/schweitzer-facts.html>, (12 October 2015).

6.  Veerle De Bock, *Building Cathedrals, the Secret Meaning of Work*, 28 October 2014, <http://www.chancestochange.com/building-cathedrals-the-secret-of-meaningful-work/> (9 June 2015).

7.  Randy Pausch, *The Last Lecture*, (New York, NY, 2008), 51-52.

8.  Jay Bilas, *Toughness: Developing True Strength On and Off the Court*, (New York, NY: Penguin Publishing), 96.

9.  Jay Bilas, *Toughness: Developing True Strength On and Off the Court*, (New York, NY: Penguin Publishing), 123-126.

## Chapter Thirteen: Hitting the Wall: "What it Will Take to Finish"

1.  Philip Sites, *Death Road of Maui*, 25, January 2013, <http://weekend-roady.com/2013/01/25/death-road-of-maui/> (14 August 2015).

2.  dangerous roads, *Kahekili Highway*, <http://www.dangerousroads. org/north-america/usa/643-kahekili-highway-usa.html> (14 August 2015).

3.  The Phrase Finder, *The best laid plans of mice and men*, <http://www.phrases.org.uk/meanings/the-best-laid-schemes-of-mice-and-men.html> (15 August 2015).

4.  Tom Rath and Donald O. Clifton, *The Big Impact of Small Interactions*, (14 October 2004), <http://www.gallup.com/businessjournal/12916/big-impact-small-interactions.aspx> (12 August 2015).

5.  Tim Hansel, *You Gotta Keep Dancing'* (Elgin, Illinois, David C. Cook Publishing Company, 1985), 21-29.

6.  Ibid, 141.

7.  Stephen Covey, *The 8th Habit* (New York, New York, Free Press, 2004), 86.

8.  Medical Dictionary, *fatigue*, <http://medical-dictionary.thefreedictionary.com/fatigue> (13 August 2015).

9.  Michael M. Lombardo and Robert W. Exchanger, *The Career Architect Development Planner* (Minneapolis, MN, Lominger Limited, Inc., 2000), 601.

10. Tony Schwartz, *Sleep as a Competitive Advantage*, (27 June 2014), <http://dealbook.nytimes.com/2014/06/27/sleep-as-a-competitive-advantage/?_r=1>, (9 August 2015).

11. Ibid.

12. Wikipedia, *Historical Rankings of Presidents of the United States*, (5 October 2015), <https://en.wikipedia.org/wiki/Historical_rankings_of_Presidents_of_the_United_States>, (5 October 2015).

13. Mark E. Neely, Jr., *The Last Best Hope of Earth* (Cambridge, Massachusetts, Harvard University Press, 1993), v.

14. Mark E. Neely, Jr., *The Last Best Hope of Earth* (Cambridge, Massachusetts, Harvard University Press, 1993), v.

15. Psychologist World Editors, *Stress:Fight or Flight Response*, <http://www.psychologistworld.com/stress/fightflight.php>, (13 August 2015).

16. Mayo Clinic Editors, *Crohn's Disease*, <http://www.mayoclinic.org/diseases-conditions/crohns-disease/basics/definition/con-20032061>, (11 August 2015).

17. David J. Schwartz, World Renowned Authority on Motivation, < *http://cornerstone.wwwhubs.com/David_Schwartz.html*>, (14 August 2015).

## Chapter 14: Hazards: "Don't Miss the Warning Signs"

1. Jeffery Brown, *The Competitive Edge* (Nashville, TN: Tyndale, 2007), 120.

2. Bob Buford, *Finishing Well* (Brentwood, TN: Integrity Publishers, 2004), 37.

3. Matt Jaffe, *Getting Lost While Hiking*, <http://hiking.about.com/od/hiking-safety-advice/a/Getting-Lost-While-Hiking.htm> (18 August 2015).

4. Joel Barker, *Future Edge* (New York, NY: William Morrow and Company, Inc., 1992), 18.

5. Anna Williams, *8 Successful People Who Use Visualization*, (8 July 2015), <http://www.mindbodygreen.com/0-20630/8-successful-people-who-use-the-power-of-visualization.html> (18 August 2015).

6. Lisa Respers France, *Jim Carrey's inspiring commencement speech*, (28 May 2014), <http://www.cnn.com/2014/05/28/showbiz/celebrity-news-gossip/jim-carrey-commencement-speech/> (18 August 2015).

7.  IMDb Editors, *Fred Rogers Biography*, <http://www.imdb.com/name/nm0736872/bio?ref_=nm_ov_bio_sm> (18 August 2015).

8.  Fred Rogers National Academy of Television Arts and Science Lifetime Achievement Award, YouTube. On line video clip, <https://www.youtube.com/watch?v=Upm9LnuCBUM> (18 August 2015).

9.  IPG, *Life Comes at You Fast*, (9 November 2012), <http://www.interpublic.com/our-agencies/recent-work/strongerpost?id=1694&casename=Life+Comes+at+You+Fast> (18 August 2015).

10. *Life Comes at You Fast*, YouTube. On line video clip, <http://www.youtube.com/watch?v+xXAdkOw-xOgWhat Ads> (9 March 2015).

11. About Education Editors, *William James Biography*, <http://psychology.about.com/od/profilesofmajorthinkers/p/jamesbio.htm> (21 August 2015).

12. Bob Buford, *Game Plan* (Grand Rapids, MI: Zondervan Publishing, 1997), 87.

13. Go Comics, *Exploring Calvin & Hobbs*, 23 February 2013, <http://www.gocomics.com/calvinandhobbes/2013/02/22> (22 August 2015).

14. Erwin McManus, *About*, *<http://www.erwinmcmanus.com/#artisansoul>*, (8 October 2015).

15. Morris Schechtman, *Working Without A Net* (New York, NY: Prentice Hall Publishing, 1994), 109.

16. Dr. Martin Luther King Jr., *What is Your Life's Blueprint*, <http://www.drmartinlutherkingjr.com/whatisyourlifesblueprint.htm> (28 February 2012).

17. Gail Matthews, *Study Focuses on Strategies for Achieving Goals, Resolutions,* 5 September 2008, <http://www.dominican.edu/dominicannews/study-highlights-strategies-for-achieving-goals> (11 November 2013).

18. Richard Wiseman, *News Years Resolution Experiment,* 2 February 2008, <http://www.quirkology.com/UK/Experiment_resolution.shtml> (15 January 2015).

19. Statistic Brain Research Institute, *New Years Resolution Statistics,* 1 February 2015, <http://www.statisticbrain.com/new-years-resolution-statistics/> (11 November 2014).

**Chapter Fifteen: Breaking the Tape: "Standing on the Podium"**

1. Timothy Johnson, *Finding God in the Questions: A Personal Journey,* (Downers Grove, IL: InterVarsity Press, 2004), 185.

2. Psalm 90:12 NIV <https://www.biblegateway.com/quicksearch/?quicksearch=teach+us+to+number+our+days&qs_version=NIV> (9 October 2015).

31132728R00134

Made in the USA
San Bernardino, CA
02 March 2016